THREE MEN ON A BIKE
A Journey through Africa

THREE MEN ON A BIKE

A Journey through Africa

RORY SPOWERS

With a foreword by
BILL ODDIE

CANONGATE

First published in Great Britain in 1995
by Canongate Books Ltd 14 High Street
Edinburgh EH1 1TE

Reprinted 1996

ISBN 0 86241 542 X

British Library Cataloguing-in-Publication Data
A catalogue record for this book is available on
request from the British Library

Typeset by Palimpsest Book Production Limited,
Polmont, Stirlingshire
Printed and bound by W.S.O.Y. Finland

FOR NUNZIO AND FOR KIM

Contents

Acknowledgements

A very special thank you to The Chloride-Exide Group in the UK and Africa for their generous support throughout the trip. It would not have been possible without their assistance and we are extremely grateful.

A big thank you to Bill Oddie and Tim Brooke Taylor for their long suffering involvement as patrons and their enthusiasm for the project.

We would also like to thank the following for their kind support:

AMREF; The Les Evans Holiday Fund for terminally ill children; John Scott and Partners; Stoppers anti-smoking lozenges; The National Blankets Company of Zimbabwe; BP (Tanzania); King and Gardiner Il Hwa Korean Ginseng; The Bicycle Workshop; Timberland (UK) Ltd; Cutler and Gross; Eveready Batteries; Elida Gibbs Ltd; AGFA (UK) Ltd; Metrocolor; The Birchwood Design Company for their Pelican trailer; The Sudanese Tractor Company; The Botswana Technology Centre; Philips Electrical (Zambia) Ltd; The Leeds Camera Centre; Carradice of Nelson Ltd; Fast Forward; Liquipak; Buccaneer Inns.

Lastly, the biggest thank you of all must go to all the African people who showered us with such relentless hospitality throughout the year – we only wish we could have done more for them.

Foreword

I suppose it was partly my fault. Back in 1969, I had been working with Tim Brooke Taylor and Graeme Garden on a TV series called *Broaden Your Mind*. It was a sort of 'comedy encyclopaedia' but, by the end of the second series, we were beginning to worry that the encyclopaedia bit was beginning to outweigh the comedy. Since we were working for the BBC Light Entertainment department, this was not entirely appropriate. So it was that the three of us attempted to come up with a new concept. In fact, we ended up by combining two or three old ones: the style of cartoon and silent comedy, with a 'sitcom' storyline. The basic 'sit' of the 'com' was that we would run an agency that would 'do anything anytime'. This wasn't exactly new either. In fact, when we presented the idea to the Head of Comedy, he stopped us after a few sentences and announced: 'Well, it's one of the oldest ideas in the book ... but presumably you're going to do something different with it.' Hopefully we did. In any event, *The Goodies* ran for just over ten years.

Well, I say 'ran'. In fact, we cycled quite a lot of it. Early in the planning of the show we decided we wanted a quirky form of transport. I'm not sure who came up with the idea of a three-seater bike. If it was me, I'm sorry. Heaven knows, I've been punished for it. So were we all. It was christened the 'trandem' (a word which may or may not officially exist). When we first saw it, we were delighted. When we first tried to ride it, we were distressed. Getting on was bad enough. Pulled muscles all round. Then, if any one of us put a foot on the pedals, they would spin round and crack the others on the shins. From the very beginning we associated the trandem with pain. Having developed enough discipline to shout 'Pedals!' as a warning for Tim on the front to make the adjustment, Graeme in the middle to synchronise with him, and me (Bill) on the back to lift my feet out of the way altogether, we attempted to actually move forward. We immediately fell off. Then we got back on, tried again, and fell off again. After an hour or so, we could manage to cycle a few yards, but whenever we stopped we almost invariably keeled over.

Agony and embarrassment are often the parents of invention. Accepting that we were probably never going to be able to ride the trandem with any degree of control, we resolved that our incompetence would become part of the comedy. Over the years, we got very good at falling off . . . in a funny way. Ironically, by the early '80's – when the series was laid to rest – we were capable of riding for several hundred yards. But I don't think we ever got to really enjoy it. In subsequent years, whenever we were asked what we missed about doing *The Goodies*, we could easily think of many things, but the trandem was definitely NOT one of them.

The same could not be said for the public. I recall once reading an article about the '70's 'revival' – it's terrible when you become nostalgia! – in which there was a list of period 'icons'. The trandem was one of them. Not us, mind you, the trandem. This unnatural obsession is supported by the fact that the question we get asked most to this very day is: 'Whatever happend to the three seater bike?'

For several years I had no answer to that one. We had heard a rumour that the BBC had auctioned it off, presumably to raise money to build some more offices for their accountants (Oops! Bit of satire there). Apparently some undergraduates had bought it. Well, they would, wouldn't they? WE were undergraduates once ourselves, so we knew what stupid things they do. We were simply amused that the trandem was out there injuring someone else. Then, in 1989, we were re-united with the infernal machine. Well, at least Tim and I were. Graeme had by this time fulfilled the long looming threat to get a 'proper job', and was therefore too busy doing something dignified to be able to accept an offer of a boozy lunch with a bunch of 'Bohemians', somewhere in Chelsea. Exactly who they all were, we never did really work out. We did however glean that at least three of them were intending to ride the length of Africa, for charity (why the hell else would one do such a thing!') on – yes – the Goodies' trandem. And there it was. After nearly ten years, it was like being faced with an old enemy. Or maybe an ex-wife from a particularly acrimonious divorce. Old hatreds were immediately rekindled. Especially when Tim and I attempted to mount it. It had now acquired a cross-bar at exactly the right height to endanger my crotch, and various other reinforcements had rendered it twice as heavy, and therefore even more lethal when it keeled over. Fortunately, our pain was dulled by a copious supply of a rather cheeky red wine. As we contorted, grinned, grimaced and reminisced, Rory Spowers explained exactly why they were taking these 'publicity photos'.

As we listened, we began to appreciate that, though the motto of the Goodies may have been 'we do anything anytime', we had never done anything as daring as these lads were about to attempt; and possibly nothing as daft! Fighting giant kittens or being clobbered with black puddings was a doddle compared with this. Nevertheless, to be honest, I felt somewhat envious as Rory explained their intended route. When I'd left Cambridge University in 1963, I had had every intention of travelling and 'seeing the world', particularly in search of wildlife. There is, of course, no better place to do that than Africa. However, as things had turned out, 'show business' had sort of 'taken over'. We'd been very successful, and I could only be grateful, but at the same time I had always rather regretted not going on some kind of major once-in-a-lifetime expedition. This was exactly what Rory and his companions were about to do.

As Tim and I left, wishing them good luck, I couldn't help but allow myself one of THE classic lines:

'God, I wish I were coming with you.'

Then I looked at the trandem.

'Perhaps not. Maybe I'll just wait for the book to come out.'

Well, here it is.

BILL ODDIE

The Journey

On one point we were all agreed, and that was that, come what might, we would go through with this job to the bitter end. If it killed us! – well, that would be a sad thing for friends and relations, but it could not be helped.

Jerome K. Jerome, *Three Men in a Boat*

Distances are only the relation of space to time and vary with that relation.

Marcel Proust, *Remembrance of Things Past*

I wanna go out in the countryside
Oh sit by the clear, cool, crystal water
Get my spirit, way back to the feeling
Deep in my soul, I wanna feel
Oh so close to the One, close to the One . . .

Can you feel the silence? Can you feel the silence?

Van Morrison, 'Hymns to the Silence'

The Goodloid

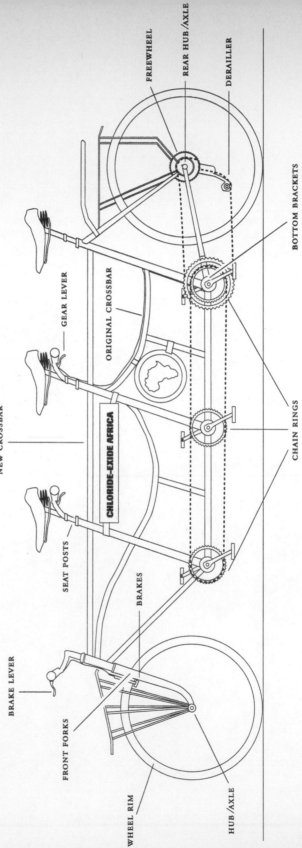

FREEWHEEL

REAR HUB/AXLE

DERAILLER

BOTTOM BRACKETS

GEAR LEVER

ORIGINAL CROSSBAR

CHAIN RINGS

NEW CROSSBAR

CHLORIDE-EXIDE AFRICA

SEAT POSTS

BRAKES

BRAKE LEVER

FRONT FORKS

WHEEL RIM

HUB/AXLE

And then there were three
. . . or four?

Blairhall is a grey stone house near the village of Culross – about twenty minutes' drive across the Forth from Edinburgh. It is not a large stately residence as the name might suggest and was rented by some friends during my last year at university for ten pounds a week. It was bare and cold but pulsated with atmosphere; a magnetic pagan aura seemed to course through the stone, and twin pyramid peaks sat on the gateposts, silhouetted against the rising moon like ancient antennae. Time did weird things at the Blair – hours and minutes became indistinguishable as you were captivated by what was referred to as 'the vortex'.

One wet evening in the spring of 1988, I was enjoying dinner in the vortex when Dave Elliott, one of my more enthusiastic friends, started bombarding me with his latest scheme.

'What are you going to do after university, man?' he asked boisterously.

'Dunno really. What about you?'

'Well, I rode this mountain bike of Black John's last weekend and thought I might ride one through Africa.'

'Oh right. Why don't we do it together on the Goodies' trandem – you know my brother bought it from an auction of BBC props a few years ago?'

'That's it man – the Goodies' trandem.' Dave jumped up and started pacing round the room, smoking with intent. His obsession was born.

It *was* a serious suggestion and I soon realised that I was not going to be able to extricate myself very easily. Dave had made up his mind. By the end of the evening we had explored the idea from every angle, ideas becoming increasingly ambitious as the wine flowed and the vortex gathered momentum.

'We can easily get sponsored, do it for charity, call it "Three Men on a Bike", make a film and write a book.' . . .

As it transpired, it was virtually impossible to get sponsored, we raised nearly ten thousand pounds for charity, we called it 'Three Men on a Bike', we sort of made a film and here I am trying to write a book.

Over the next few months we discussed the idea relentlessly; how many other people should be involved, if any, and who. I remained as non-committal as possible. The acid house boom was in its infancy and I was making good money selling dayglo surf shorts which I had imported from Thailand. By September however, I was sick of the rag trade; Africa bounced into the forefront of my mind and my commitment was made.

Our first problem was which charity to support. Dave approached the Les Evans Holiday Fund for Terminally Ill Children after seeing one of their posters in a pub. Les Evans suffered from polio earlier in his life and set up a charity in 1976 to send terminally ill children on once-in-a-lifetime holidays to Disneyland and Disneyworld. The fund relies purely on donations and is run by a jovial bearded man called Peter Hawkins. Unfortunately Les has died since then – he was a man with compassion engraved in his small rounded face; somebody who had suffered, but survived through strength of heart and soul.

After some research AMREF – The African Medical Research Foundation – seemed the most appropriate charity which would be of benefit to the majority of our host countries, and we co-ordinated a meeting with their Director, Elizabeth Young, in the Upper Richmond Road. (AMREF is based in Nairobi and operates throughout East Africa; they run the Flying Doctor service and in recent years have done extensive research into AIDS and into controlling the spread of malaria.) I was hungover that morning, after a friend's birthday, and Dave virtually had to lift me onto the bike. Once in the confines of an austere office, I got worse and worse, my head pounding and swimming with thick liquid brain. I only spoke once throughout the ordeal, a sort of garbled grunt which caused a slight pause before being brushed aside. Dave managed to keep boring on and the meeting concluded amicably, agreeing to split the funds raised equally between the two organisations.

Dave and I spent a few remarkably unconstructive weekends trying to formulate an overall plan. On the first of these we sat down in front of a large sheet of paper to draw a flow-chart; a few hours later we still had one box at the top announcing in strident black capitals – THE IDEA. Another piece of paper listed umpteen suggestions of what should flow from THE IDEA but we never managed to solve the chicken and egg dilemma of how to get the ball rolling. One weekend I was presented with our first brochure – a piece of A4 which dramatically heralded *The Cape to Cairo Dream* and advocated a twenty-thousand-kilometre route through equatorial rainforest and the Sahara. It was unbelievably pompous drivel, stuffed with quotations from Lawrence and references to *the quaternion*. At this time we realised that it would be a step in the right direction to actually locate the trandem. Dave had never set eyes on it and I'd had the chance to ride it round the block once, about two years before.

Alan P— has a collection of bizarre bicycles; for some reason he always wears a black glove on his right hand. He is affected rather than eccentric, and can often be spotted weaving through Chelsea traffic on a penny farthing. My brother Hugo first met him outside Hamley's toy shop trying to buy a trailer for a Sinclair C5. Alan had borrowed the trandem for a while and we met at his flat in Battersea to retrieve her. With considerable difficulty we manoeuvred all ten feet out of his basement, up some stairs and onto the road. At this stage she had no gears, two ancient and very buckled wheels, some semblance of a braking system on the front and no crossbar on the frame; even the slightest corner sent tremors through the flexing metal as it threatened to break in half.

We set off round the block amidst ominous creaking sounds and general hysteria. This initial run did little to dissuade us. On the contrary it fuelled our enthusiasm and prompted the first steps towards her renovation. A few telephone calls revealed the existence of The Tandem Shop in the Old Kent Road. This had to be the right place and the next day I set off on a perilous journey across London to entrust the bike to these specialists for a complete overhaul – new brakes, new wheels and a ten-speed derailleur system. Over the next fortnight I rang up to check on the progress; he seemed to be having difficulty fitting a drive system and asked for more time. I agreed and waited a week before ringing again. For several days there was no reply and at the weekend Dave and I went to investigate. We found the shop boarded up and deserted except for the tandem lying upside down and in lots of pieces. A little research in the pub opposite revealed that the shop and everything in it was now the property of the liquidators and that the owner had disappeared. Alarmed by this development we explained our situation to a passing policeman; he helpfully recommended 'leaning heavily against the door'. We were about to follow this advice when a spare key was produced from a second hand shop next door and we were reunited with what was now referred to as 'The Goodloid' (the result of some peculiar slang developed in Edinburgh, whereby the suffix '-loid' was added onto the end of key words).

December came and we had still been unable to convince anybody that we were serious. For some time we considered doing it by ourselves with a plastic dummy on the middle seat. Various friends showed interest but were tied by demanding girlfriends and career prospects. In the first week of December we took our swelling collection of badly typed brochures and a few maps, and headed down to Peckham Rye to, as Dave explained, 'zap Chris with the sirens'. Dave had known Chris Mills since childhood. A wiry, resilient character with a broad smile, Chris seemed to contain a brooding intensity behind his mild mannered extension. As I would discover his relaxed attitude hides high tensile nerves of steel and an unwavering stamina. Chris had witnessed Dave's skinhead stage, directed his love of weapons away from butterfly knives towards *nunchukkas* (Bruce Lee-style batons tied together by a piece of chain) and had been a regular visitor to Blairhall. Parental pressure had driven him towards gainful employment and for the last few months he had been living in Streatham and working for a south London estate agent. We found him sitting at a very empty desk reading a copy of the *Sun* in an office which looked like it had failed to sell a house in several years. Dragging him to the pub, we hit him with two pints and a tirade of reasons as to why he should leave his job and come to Africa. Within twenty-four hours he had convinced himself; convincing his girlfriend proved more difficult.

Two weeks later I discovered that Steve Corry, an old school-friend, was painting another friend's house in the Lillie Road. Known to some as 'the tousle-haired hobo', Steve was one of my greatest friends. We had slightly lost touch during university years but previous exploits dated back to our inter-rail experiences when we were sixteen. Apart from the occasional controlled tantrum which one expects from a Gemini, he is philosophical, pensive and extremely mellow. Immediately I decided that he had to come. A fourth person now seemed crucial, especially since I was obsessed with trying to film the trip; the visual impact of the trandem would be completely lost without three people on board. Also a support vehicle of some kind seemed sensible and Dave already had a mountain bike. In any case I felt apprehensive about three people travelling together; a fourth person would make relationships a bit easier.

'Steve? Hi, it's Rory – how's it going?'

'OK. I'm painting Tom's house at the moment.'

'So I hear – are you doing anything for lunch?'

'Well, I was going to make some soup actually.'

'Right – we're coming in low.'

Within half an hour we were busy advocating the myriad merits of cycling the Goodies' trandem across Africa. Steve needed little convincing; he put down his paintbrush and with characteristic calm said:

'Sure – as long as I can bring my guitar.'

This spontaneous decision took the wind out of our sails slightly.

'You don't have to decide now – mull it over for a couple of days if you want.'

'No, it's cool – I want to come.'

The restoration saga continued. Bike UK in Clapham charged

us one hundred and fifty pounds for fitting a Sturmey Archer hub which broke within two hundred yards. This was double the original estimate and a heated confrontation ensued. In recompense we received two forty-eight spoke wheels built round Isuzu hubs which went on to cover six thousand miles without a problem. The drive system continued to present problems; nothing could withstand the weight and power of three people tearing back home from the pub – chain rings bent double, hubs disintegrated and bearings were liberally dispensed to the London roads in small powdered particles. By Christmas we had discovered the only bicycle shop in London prepared to take up the challenge of updating what we now knew to be a 1930s frame – The Bicycle Workshop in Notting Hill's infamous All Saints Road.

Tom Board strengthened the frame with a crossbar, while Ninon Lauritz and her assistant Martin struggled to find obsolete bottom brackets and a gear system which would last more than a couple of days. In the New Year we had the first semblance of a functional Goodloid, but the next three months proved to be a continual rejigging as we systematically fitted and destroyed the strongest tandem parts available. This became very expensive. Eventually we commissioned an engineering student at London University to build a set of chain rings out of high-tensile steel; he broke four machining tools in the process but did produce the ultimate state-of-the-art parts.

Chris, Dave and I moved into a flat at 333 King's Road in the New Year, 1989. My brother had recently bought it from an extremely suspect Libyan, who had lived there with several wives and a multitude of children. It was far from what one might expect a Chelsea flat to look like; the carpets were covered in huge stains where food had been cooked over a Bunsen burner; mattresses had other more dubious stains and structural maintenance was long overdue. However, at thirty pounds a week nobody was going to complain. The drawing room became the Three Men on a Bike (TMOAB) office – a chaotic hive of activity with maps all over the walls and reggae records mingling with bicycle tools and a sea of paperwork all over the floor.

The telephone confusion shed new light on the previous tenant. First we discovered that there were three different lines and the only one that worked was a direct line to my bedroom. About this time the newspapers were full of the Pamela Bordes affair and her association with Ahmed Gaddaf – Gaddafi's right hand man. Over this period I was woken on several occasions by the telephone ringing in the middle of the night and each time I received a long-distance muffled voice asking for Ahmed. For a while we had visions of the SAS crashing through our windows or of Libyan terrorists trying to blow us up.

The fact that the telephone was up a flight of stairs and in my bedroom was particularly inconvenient. Everyone would be assembled in the office scripting their hundredth begging letter of the day; a break in the music would reveal the faint murmur of the telephone and somebody would sprint off down the passage, spurred on by shouts of 'Get it man, that's somebody offering us ten grand.' Even if you did get the phone in time you had tremendous difficulty in making anybody understand what you were saying due to some problem with the mouthpiece – you either sounded like you had an appalling cold or were sitting in an empty bath. Trying to make a prospective sponsor understand what you were all about was hard enough anyway. It was especially hard if they had never heard of the Goodies because one had to then explain at great length about the bike and its history. Even if you managed to get this all across to a secretary she would frequently assume that you were completely insane, laugh nervously and forget all about you.

Dave invented a very successful tactic. He wrote a series of absurdly idiotic letters to all the suncream and deodorant manufacturers, hoping that if he managed to be foolish enough, then somebody might reply. It was the most efficient strategy to date; by April we had amassed enough suncream and deodorant to last a lifetime.

Another method was the 'cold call'. This was usually instigated when everybody was very bored and not knowing what to do next. A game of spoof would decide who had to ring up a company and ask them directly for some of their products. (Spoof was to become an obligatory ritual to select someone for any really unpleasant task.

It entails guessing the total number of coins held in the outstretched right hands of the players, a correct guess releasing you from the torment of the next round.) Everyone else would assemble round the telephone, put on plastic policemen's hats and leap about trying to distract the unfortunate loser. Surprisingly this actually worked on a few occasions; Cutler and Gross invited us to choose sunglasses and Timberland provided us each with a pair of boots.

Mr Cutler and Mr Gross run a very smart opticians in Knightsbridge, where they design very expensive sunglasses for the stars. Three Men on a Bike wandered in one morning and announced themselves to the girl behind the desk. 'Ah yes – why don't you look round and choose.' For fifteen minutes we dithered around trying on all the most expensive specs in the shop. Rather vague about what to do next, I presented a pair of sixty-five pound sunglasses to the counter and sheepishly said 'I'd rather like these please.' 'Certainly sir,' was her reply before putting them in a case and handing them back to me. I had never been in a position to walk into a shop before, pick up something expensive and walk out again without paying; it felt very good indeed.

Before Christmas Dave and I had written to all the cycle courier companies in London offering to work for them on the trandem as an advertising gimmick. The boss of Cyclone Couriers at the time was a Mr Odd; as I wrote the envelope, I'd said to Dave 'I bet he gives us a job'. Sure enough in the New Year we found ourselves tearing hazardously around the West End working for Mr Odd. Our first job was picking up something from Capital Radio on the Euston Road. I was sitting on the back wearing Dr Who's eight-yard tailcoat, which Hugo had bought at the same time as the trandem; the eight-yards were stuffed into my courier bag along with a silver platter. I walked into the foyer bearing the silver platter, while Dave carried the end of the tailcoat like a bridesmaid walking down the aisle. We placed our package on the tray, swivelled round and wandered out. The drop-off was some building in the West End – on the third floor. We found ourselves trying to negotiate a network of long corridors – I had to work my way through swing doors and round corners with Dave stumbling along eight yards behind trying to extricate bustling secretaries from my tails. This caused so much confusion that we decided to ditch the 'Exclusive Silver Platter Service'.

Steve continued to live in the Lillie Road with Tom. One day he suggested that we have some publicity shots taken by A—, a successful portrait photographer and friend of Tom's. A— is middle-aged, gay and lives in a Kensington mews. A date was fixed with Bill Oddie and Tim Brooke-Taylor to come for lunch at 333 before the shoot, but Bill had a busy schedule so we agreed to meet him at A—'s house if he could not make lunch. On the day bottles of rosé and stories from Tim made us forget the time. We arrived at A—'s house to find Bill and his wife suffering the inane banter of a fat old queen quoting Oscar Wilde, while a never-ending parade of pretty, blond public schoolboys streamed in and out of the house. I think Bill and Tim might have subsequently formulated a rather disturbing impression of what Three Men on a Bike was all about. With extreme difficulty we manoeuvred the Goodloid into the ground-floor studio and got on with the shoot, Bill and Tim keeping everybody amused with their spontaneous rapport.

The route we were to take through Africa went through several changes. South Africa was one problem; the trip had always been intended to stretch from the Cape to Cairo. Despite our unanimous hatred for the fascist regime, we felt it was part of the distance and should be included. As time went by it became increasingly obvious that we should not go. A major sponsor had pulled out after learning that South Africa was on the agenda and countries further north turned you away if they knew that you had been there. We could get round this by having the stamp put on a loose leaf in our passports, but we would have to sustain the lie throughout the media coverage which we had promised our sponsors. Dave had been born in South Africa but his passport only listed Durban as his birthplace; if ever questioned about this at borders in Africa he would have to explain that it was a village called Durban in Sussex not Durban, South Africa.

From Botswana to Kenya the planned route remained quite constant, except for a short phase when Dave insisted that we should go through eastern Zaire, Burundi, Rwanda and Uganda.

From Kenya to northern Sudan was the major problem. Research into the existence of tarmac on the four-thousand-mile route through Central Africa made it clear that we would be pushing the trandem a very long way. The solution was to fly from Nairobi to Khartoum, using our sponsorship money in Kenya to buy the flights. It was quite a distance to miss but we consoled ourselves with the thought that the stretch we would be doing through Europe, from Milan to London, was of a similar length.

We aimed to leave on April Fool's Day. By mid-March it was patently obvious that this was impossible. Hannah Wood, a friend of Hugo's in PR, negotiated with various airlines on our behalf for sponsored flights. We were led to believe that Air Zaire were keen to fly us free to Kinshasa and Steve decided to take the matter into his own hands.

'Hello, Air Zaire?'

'Yes.'

'Ah hello, my name is Steve Corry from Three Men on a Bike. I understand that you have very kindly offered us free flights and I was wondering when I might come and collect the tickets.'

A bewildered secretary put Steve through to her boss. Steve tried the same spiel but cut no ice with an irritated managing director.

'What do you mean – we never offered anything.'

We eventually secured cut-price tickets with free passage for the Goodloid on British Airways. A departure date was fixed – 28th April – Dave's twenty-third birthday.

Chloride Exide had emerged as our best hope for a main sponsor. We had received five hundred pounds from Stoppers anti-smoking lozenges, free batteries from Eveready, film from Agfa, cycle panniers from Carradice, our trailer from Pelican, Timberland boots, Cutler and Gross sunglasses and a stockpile of suncream and deodorant. However, we still needed money to live on for a year and, with factories throughout Africa, Chloride Exide became a prime target for our pitch.

Steve was banned from coming to the first meeting because his hair was too long, something he still cannot believe. We shuffled in looking incongruous in second-hand, badly fitting suits. Things looked promising in every country except Botswana, Tanzania and Sudan, where they did not operate. Local currency could be arranged in Zimbabwe, Zambia, Malawi, Kenya and Egypt in return for publicity in the local media. We itemised what we needed in each country on the basis of five pounds per person per day and figures were agreed upon a week later. Two weeks before leaving however, we were told the deal was off. A series of diplomatic but slightly aggressive phone-calls followed, fortunately maintaining some semblance of the arrangement. The original seven thousand pounds was cut dramatically to three thousand three hundred. We would receive one thousand in sterling before we left and about five hundred pounds' worth of local currency in each of five countries where they had factories.

Our one and only trial run on the Goodloid was to Oxford for a radio interview. We covered over eighty miles in the day and felt totally shattered. Fitness had been approached in a half-hearted fashion – a few skirmishes around Battersea Park and some apathetic visits to the multi-gym at Chelsea Baths. We were cycling everywhere in London however – to all our meetings in the day and often at night. Dave and I operated an informal taxi service, carefully selecting possible passengers from the pavement. One unsuspecting Swedish girl asked us where the Hippodrome was. Before she knew what was happening we were tearing through the Hyde Park underpass and up Piccadilly with this poor girl precariously clinging to the middle seat. On another occasion Dave and his younger brother spent most of a Saturday evening with a bagpiper playing on the back after he had accosted them on the King's Road. Moonlit trips through the park became popular until I steered three of us into a lake.

In our bid to tackle the myriad of things left to do, Dave appointed himself 'equipment manager' about a month before we left. I pursued friends of friends for unused film stock lying redundant in Soho fridges, sought advice on sound equipment and pestered TV producers for backing. Chris and Steve kept churning out letters to everyone from Richard Branson to merchant bankers.

One evening Dave and I took the trandem down to Vauxhall to see Desmond Dekker and the Aces. During the gig I suggested that we should try and book him for a party in a bid to raise money for the two charities. Afterwards we approached the band, told them about the trip and got the manager's number. The next morning we booked a venue called Crazy Larry's off the King's Road and made a series of calls to Desmond's management, trying to knock his fee down as much as possible. I got him down to five hundred pounds and the departure party was set. We printed up fliers and for the next week distributed them over central London. The actual day was hectic. We had to bring in a sound system, monitors and a mixing desk; Steve was given a crash course in sound engineering and we waited nervously to see if the man himself would appear. By ten o'clock we had over four hundred people in but none of them was Desmond Dekker. At ten thirty he showed, the bottle of Rémy Martin requested on the rider was presented and he was onstage at eleven. Five hundred sweaty people skanked solidly for an hour. The bar tab was four times higher than the limit we had to guarantee and we had raised eight hundred pounds for charity at the door. The manager of the club had promised to make a donation if it was a good night, but now refused.

Departure day dawned. My stomach swarmed with butterflies, denying me food. I had been so involved with camera lenses, stock tests and Wratten 85 filters that I had overlooked buying any clothes for Africa. I did some frantic shopping, buying jeans and a silk shirt, and stuffed my pannier full: a treasured red, yellow and green towel, a sponge-bag, a jersey, thick socks, two pairs of shorts, two T-shirts, cassettes, sunglasses and an old edition of *The Cape to Cairo* written by E.S. Grogan after he had walked the length of Africa a century before I was trying to cycle it. Reading it, I discovered that he was actually carried a large proportion of the way, usually in the throes of high fever, by his vast retinue of slaves. The book is basically a catalogue of his fanatical hunting exploits and I surmised that he had shot most of the elephants in Africa. The only real correlation between his experiences and ours was the never-ending plight of malaria which he seemed to get every other day for five years.

Our flight was at seven in the evening from Gatwick. Our deadline for leaving the flat was three, needing plenty of time to check the bikes in and say our goodbyes. At four there was still no sign of Steve, I was still packing, Dave had lost his sunglasses and pandemonium reigned. Steve soon appeared, his hair cut short and apologised that he was late because he had been finishing making tapes – of which he had eighteen. Ten minutes later he had lost his plane ticket, I was trying to film our departure and Dave was still looking for his precious new sunglasses. Chris had made the wise choice of driving to Gatwick with his girlfriend. Pandemonium turned to panic until Steve realised that his ticket had been in his pocket all the time. Dave was forced to forget about his sunglasses and at four thirty we cycled off from a small crowd of close friends to get the train from Victoria to Gatwick. It was the weirdest feeling that I had ever known, an overload of different emotions stewing in nervous adrenalin. On the train things relaxed. We drank a can of 6X each, sat down between carriages and felt almost normal. At Gatwick we created chaos weaving the trandem, trailer and mountain bike through the crowds, in and out of lifts and trains and up and down escalators. The check-in desk thought we were joking. We explained that we were very serious and were flying to Botswana. A senior official was summoned and he confirmed it, explaining how we must prepare the Goodloid for her voyage.

Formalities dealt with, we joined families and friends in the bar. Les Evans and Peter Hawkins had very kindly come to see us off and bought us our last English pint for a year. Passing through the barrier to board the plane I wondered whether this trip would prove to be the worst decision of my life – half an hour later this anxiety had been dissipated by waves of excitement and feelings of freedom.

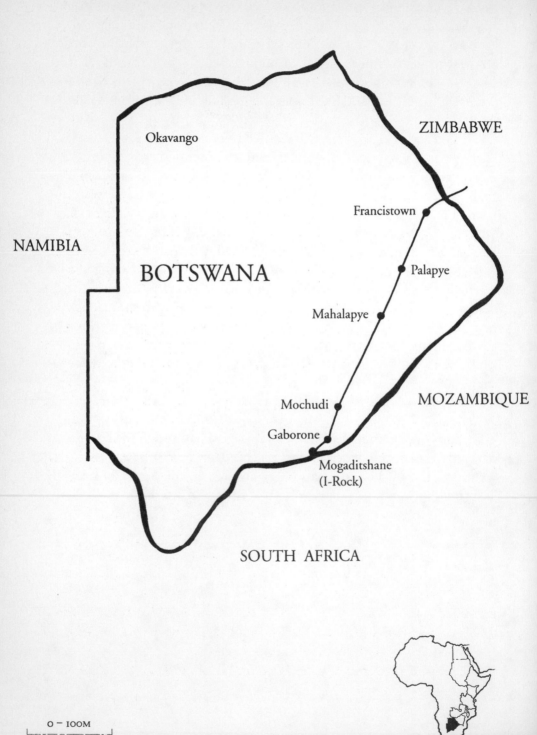

ZIMBABWE

Okavango

NAMIBIA

BOTSWANA

Francistown

Palapye

Mahalapye

MOZAMBIQUE

Mochudi

Gaborone

Mogaditshane
(I-Rock)

SOUTH AFRICA

O – 100M
APPROX. SCALE

Botswana

As we began our descent to Seretse Khama airport, I grappled with the thought that the distance we had just covered in a few hours was going to take nearly a year on the way back. We caught our first glimpse of African soil and acquainted ourselves with the burnt russet bushland, wide horizons and clear azure skies which were going to become so familiar. Four miniatures of Cognac found their way to four exhilarated faces as rubber screeched onto tarmac.

Gaborone's airport is not a big place and a representative from the British High Commission had little difficulty in spotting TMOAB as we shuffled through Immigration, clad in floral shirts provided by Stephen King, a designer in the King's Road. Having been refused sponsorship by Barclays Bank on the basis that they 'no longer operated in Africa', I was somewhat irritated by a massive advertisement boldly pronouncing 'Barclays Bank Welcomes You to Botswana'. Our bank manager in London fell even further in our estimation.

The young man from the High Commission greeted us and helped smooth over any trouble created by the trandem appearing at customs on the conveyor belt, and we soon found ourselves outside on the tarmac, trying to revert both bicycles to a roadworthy condition. Tyres had been deflated for the flight, pedals removed and handlebars twisted through ninety degrees. Half an hour later we embarked on our first ride under African skies. Within four hundred yards we had broken down. The trailer tyres had not been deflated for the flight and the pressurisation had severely distorted one tyre, causing it to bump up and down on every revolution.

Our spirited behaviour towards the end of the flight had drawn us to the attention of an English woman two rows behind. She was visiting her daughter, who was married to a white South African architect living in the bush outside Gaborone. She was busy recounting our exploits and intentions to them in their Land Rover, when she saw us standing at the roadside, with both bicycles and the trailer turned upside down. We were busy convincing ourselves that a log in the long grass was not actually a lion but a paranoid delusion; that we had proceeded only four hundred yards along our six thousand five hundred-mile route was not deemed an issue for discussion. The Land Rover pulled up alongside.

'Where are you heading?' asked the driver.

'Cairo,' was the enthusiastic reply from the roadside, as we struggled in vain to make the tyre look circular again.

They kindly offered us a place to camp by their house at Mogaditshane, about twelve kilometres outside Gaborone, drawing us a map to explain the network of paths through the bush. Thanking them, we resumed our attempt to cover the remaining ten kilometres to town.

A football match had just finished at Gaborone stadium and the entire population seemed to be pouring onto the streets and returning home. We assumed that it had been a very dull game because everybody looked extremely quiet and despondent, hardly registering the bizarre spectacle that drifted past them towards the golf club. We had been given a rather tenuous contact at the last minute in London and were seeking him out at the clubhouse. Mr Reg Richardson was helping a few beetroot faces prop up the bar as we sheepishly introduced ourselves. I got the feeling that our shambolic explanation of who we were and what we were up to went in one ear and out the other, but he eagerly invited us to help demolish cans of Olssen's Lager which were being offered free that day as a promotion. Over a can or two we decided to buy some food, head out to the bush and take up the invitation of somewhere to camp.

About nine kilometres south of Gaberone, we turned off the tarmac and onto a gravel road leading to the village of Habane. Soon we developed more trailer trouble, the corrugations, ruts and bumps turning it over every two hundred yards. This gravel turned to dirt trails which would demand care in a four-wheel drive. Recent rains had created huge puddles to negotiate and, as the light faded, we were left floundering in the bush.

Eventually we stumbled across our hosts. Paul was a brilliant young architect who had moved to Botswana, partly in reaction to the South African regime, but also to take advantage of Botswana's prosperous economy and booming construction industry. He lived with his wife Vivienne and her daughter Georgina in a series of elaborate mud huts he had built on a plot of several acres. He had used local materials throughout, except for huge pieces of tarpaulin which formed the outer layer on the roofs, draped diagonally across the main crossbeam and held at adjacent corners by giant guy-ropes and tent pegs. The rooms stayed cool in the hot season due to gaps between the top of the walls and the tarpaulin, but also seemed relatively waterproof during the rains which now fell relentlessly through the night. There was no moon so, in total darkness, Paul showed us to a sheltered area a few hundred yards from his house, where a cluster of boulders formed a rocky outcrop about thirty metres high, surrounded by cultivated fields. Some trees provided shelter and we started to pitch our tents over the long grass. With customary lack of foresight we had failed to practise erecting our tents before leaving England. As the rain gathered momentum we struggled to put poles together in pitch darkness, trying to ascertain exactly what they should look like.

This became our camp for the next two weeks and for some inexplicable reason was referred to as I-Rock. The rains continued to appear at night, but during the day we enjoyed the warm, clear African winter. The trailer had made its point very quickly – progress was going to be slow if it insisted on turning over every few hundred yards. The fundamental problem was that we had an absurd amount of stuff. In addition to 16 mm film equipment and stock, a tape machine and thirty-five cassettes, a complete fishing kit and a guitar, we had a range of Streamlite torches, the largest of which was two feet long and weighed several kilos, a very expensive multi-fuel cooker which never worked, a stack of Steve's guitar books and enough clothing for an expedition to the South Pole. This had led us to construct a wire mesh cage on top of the trailer to accommodate four sleeping bags and two cumbersome tents.

Over dinner on the first night, Paul suggested approaching the Botswana Technology Centre to build us a more appropriate trailer. The next morning we appeared at the BTC and explained ourselves; it transpired that they were trying to develop a cycle trailer anyway and they seemed only too delighted to design something to our specifications in exchange for our Pelican (it was wanted for transporting pigs' stomachs!). Plans were drawn up for something large enough to accommodate the guitar and all our equipment and over the next two weeks we watched our new trailer take shape. A vast framework of angle-iron was covered with boards of 6 mm plywood and supported over two very standard wheels. It was big enough for one of us to sit inside and close the lid, and after pulling it two hundred yards down the road we had concluded that it was 'absolutely perfect'.

The delights of Gaborone supermarkets were quite a discovery – genuine Barilla pasta and fillet steak at two pounds per kilo. I was surprised by what was available but it exemplified the relative affluence of a country which purports to have the highest foreign reserve of any country in Africa – purely due to the enormous stockpile of diamonds which they cannot put on the market for another twenty years without completely destroying the equilibrium. The city itself is small, a cluster of concrete skyscrapers soaring out of the flat monotonous bushland, juxtaposed with modern residential housing on a grid pattern. The *pula* is a hard currency so a black market is non-existent. The major tourist attraction, the Okavango Swamps, has come to be regarded as one of the best game reserves in Africa and prices have been adjusted accordingly to tap the wealthy American on safari. Any aspirations of going to Okavango were soon quelled; a few days there would have halved our budget for the year.

Trips into town became more of a burden than a buzz, the majority of our time being spent in the bush, undergoing what we called our 'acclimatisation' – essentially a time of trying to familiarise ourselves with this alien environment, learn how to put up our tents, how to work our cooker and to increase our limited grasp of cycle maintenance. One day Chris was left on guard at I-Rock while the rest of us went to town. When we returned he informed us that 'some weird things happened' while we were away.

A half-crazed local, with a penchant for practising karate manoeuvres, had stumbled across our camp. He took great pleasure in demonstrating his Bruce Lee impersonation for Chris, especially when he discovered his very long and very sharp filleting knife. Within seconds he had succeeded in virtually severing his thumb, prompting Chris to use half our medical kit to patch him up. At this stage a large snake had slithered out of my tent and into view. The karate kid immediately wanted to kill it and a mad scene ensued as the two of them chased the snake around the camp. Chris used to catch snakes when working on farms in Australia; he wanted to see it gone but had no desire to kill it. His new friend however, was determined. Chris was a few feet away clutching a pronged stick, when the snake reared up and showered his face with venom. Spitting cobras are notoriously accurate, especially from such a short distance, and it is fairly miraculous that his eyes were untouched. Venom in the eyes can have serious consequences – they literally swell up and without treatment can burst apart, leaving you blind. Chris wiped the venom from his face and looked on as his lunatic accomplice bashed the living daylights out of the snake with a club and threw it behind a rock.

Chris took us through the sequence of events with characteristic calm, while we listened in horror. I was far from comfortable about sleeping with an antagonised cobra in the area and went to check that is was actually dead. Peering down a crack in the rocks I saw the huge pulsating body looking very much alive. Chris spent the next half-hour trying to stab it through the head with the filleting knife attached to a stick while Dave pointed a torch down the crack. Steve and I hovered round the fire wondering if this sort of thing was going to happen every day.

Fortunately this was our only visit from the karate kid, but we did see a lot of two other characters – Boiki and Godfrey. Boiki owned some land nearby which he supposedly farmed; in fact I think his wife farmed it while Boiki patronised the local bars. He was affable, amusing and unbelievably lazy. He informed us that snakes symbolise the ancestor spirits and that Chris's encounter had been a visitation. We never quite deduced whether killing it was an unspeakably bad omen or not. Godfrey was the local 'cool dude', complete with tie-dye jeans, black wraparound shades and a denim waistcoat covered in patches. He spoke good English, revelled in listening to our tapes and loved having his photograph taken.

The second memorable intrusion at I-Rock happened one evening while Dave and I were cooking butternuts over a kitchen fire, having given up on our stove. Two soldiers suddenly appeared from the bush behind us, carrying automatic weapons and demanding passports. As we relayed their arrival to the other two, the rest of the platoon appeared out of the darkness. About twenty soldiers had surrounded I-Rock believing us to be South African insurgents. We rapidly produced our passports and stared at the array of hardware before us – machine-guns, night-sights and rocket launchers. After burbling as much as we could about three-man bikes and a journey to Cairo we were left in peace. However, we had been joined that evening by a South African who had jumped bail to avoid national service and was camping in the bush nearby with friends. He kept a low profile throughout and was left quivering by the fire for the next half-hour.

These first two weeks were otherwise uneventful. It felt para-doxically natural and unreal at the same time, a sort of conflict between preconceptions. Having spent six months working towards this situation it seemed that it had evolved naturally, as if it was an inevitable progression. At the same time I would sit and meditate at the top of I-Rock, stare at the long horizons and the vast canopy of sky pulled taut to its extremities, and wonder what on earth we were all doing here. The week before leaving England had been so hectic that we never had time to sit down and evaluate what was going on. Suddenly we seemed to be at Gatwick, saying goodbye and disappearing for a year. Here in Africa, the sheer scale of space was the most penetrating first impression – I had never seen so much sky. The air tasted clean and the silence of boundless space was broken only by birdsong. Over the previous months I had acted out the trip in my dreams: I had been bitten by snakes, mauled by lions and shot by bandits. All sense of fear and innate paranoia seemed to fade on arrival; suddenly it was all happening and that was 'the deal'.

On May 14th we made our move. We crammed our mobile home into the new trailer, said goodbye to I-Rock, Paul, Vivienne and Georgina and set off towards town to pick up the road to Francistown. We had barely covered a hundred yards when I noticed that the two St Christophers I wore round my neck had disappeared. Not a very auspicious start and panic ensued, fortunately curtailed when I found them nestled in the long grass back at the camp. We paused in Gaborone to buy Tuffy Tape – a strip of strong plastic to insert between tyre and inner tube – supposedly the ultimate answer to preventing punctures.

With the blaster tied to the front rack, we headed onto the open road. Bob Marley was singing about 'Three o'clock Roadblock' when we caught sight of a barrier and some soldiers ahead. It was the first of many roadblocks and sure enough it was three o'clock on the dot. They waved us through, dissolving into laughter as we passed. We found ourselves tearing along at unprecedented speeds which I now attribute to initial excitement. It was a tremendous release to finally find ourselves staring towards a distant horizon, surrounded only by the bush. At the same time Cairo felt like it was a very long way away at the top of a very big hill.

Two nights before, Paul and Vivienne had taken us to the Bodiba Country Club, a rambling bar, sprawling across a small hill outside Gaborone. The view at dusk was spectacular, a crimson sun set over a panorama of flat bush, while a Zambian band struck up under a tree. We found ourselves talking to an eloquent middle-aged man who claimed that the chief of nearby Mochudi was his uncle. He insisted that we should stop there and present ourselves to the chief, and promised to alert him to our imminent arrival. It seemed vaguely credible and well worth pursuing; Mochudi was only thirty kilometres away and was a sensible target for the first day, assuming that we would break down several times en route. In fact the thirty kilometres went surprisingly quickly and in retrospect was one of only two days in the year without a breakdown.

As we entered Mochudi we were besieged by schoolchildren, intensely excited about our arrival. They helped us push the trailer up the hill to the chief's house where ferocious dogs chased us very rapidly back down. Somebody told us that the chief was away so we set about looking for a place to camp. A small stream wiggled its way through some lush pasture below the village – this seemed ideal and we pitched our tents by a clump of thorny scrub. The area was soon littered with more equipment than most sensible people would put in a caravan. We must have still been under the impression that we needed even more equipment because we had acquired two hurricane lamps and a new, larger cooker on the way into town. This cooker also refused to work, belching out a four-foot cone of flame like a burning oil rig.

It transpired that the chief of Mochudi was a leading figure in Botswanan tribal government and an advocate of quite radical politics. He was a staunch campaigner for cannabis legalisation and that evening we watched most of the young male population emerge from bushes behind the stream with glazed eyes and massive grins. The following morning we met two Scottish teachers who had been in Mochudi for seven years; they had initially been contracted for a year but had clearly seen the advantages of living under the chief of Mochudi's jurisdiction and found it difficult to pull themselves away. The day was spent stripping both bikes right down, greasing bearings and cleaning chains – maintenance that had proved impossible in the long grass at I-Rock. Dave also dreamt up an idea which would keep us amused for weeks to come – a selection of four facial hair types were written on pieces of paper, thrown into a hat and passed round. Dave consequently nurtured a goatee beard and moustache, progressively looking like Richard Branson. Chris got away with a conventional moustache, turning into a renegade army explorer, while Steve sprouted lamb-chop sideboards and just looked ridiculous. Perhaps the most foolish of all was the thin strip of beard which I had to cultivate in the style of Abraham Lincoln.

The next morning we aimed for an early start. Sleeping near to the stream proved to have been a mistake because at dawn everything was damp. By the time we had consumed a typically huge breakfast and agonised over trying to fit our array of belongings back into the trailer, two hours had elapsed. With hurricane lamps dangling from the back of it and unnecessary amounts of food strapped to the top, we made our way back to the road.

Before we had passed the outskirts of Mochudi, we were in trouble; one of the trailer wheels had buckled like a banana due to the weight it was being made to support. Brute force was applied to resurrect its shape and we tried again. The next twenty kilometres seemed to pass without a problem, the only worry being a disconcerting pinging noise which emanated from the front wheel every few minutes. We were still mobile so I shrugged it off as 'the frame settling into Africa'. Several kilometres and plenty of pings later, we pulled over for a break by a roadside shop. Only then did we realise that for every ping we had lost a spoke and that the front wheel was now devoid of structure. On reflection this was hardly surprising – the front rack was supporting two heavy panniers, a sleeping bag and the blaster. Trying to keep the steering straight was a serious struggle in itself and, after ten miles at the helm, your forearms felt like they had been put through rigorous exercises in a multi-gym. We tried to rearrange our belongings to take the weight off the front – the problem with this was that the rear wheel received even more of a load, squashing the tyre flat onto the tarmac.

A radical reappraisal was evidently needed. We stopped in the small railway town of Artesia and pitched our tents behind a shop run by a friendly but rather bemused woman. Everything came out: tools, spares, clothes, medical kit, fishing rods, guitar books and film equipment. I immediately wanted to dispense with the tents, something that was greeted with less enthusiasm by the others and which was to become a prime area of disagreement in the months to come. A TMOAB battle-cry was 'it never rains in Africa and if it does you can always take cover'. In a thoughtless moment I had made this naïve comment – at the first sight of rain I was never allowed to forget it.

We decided to stop bothering with cookers; the one we had now was bulky and required a separate fuel bottle which leaked everywhere with monotonous regularity. Apart from anything else it did not work so we decided to cook on open fires for as long as possible. We became quite expert at this, brewing up tea in five minutes, and never resorted to a cooker again until Tanzania when the rains made it impossible to find dry wood. In Botswana and Zimbabwe it was often easier to buy steak than anything else and lunch regularly consisted of nothing but large pieces of beef, covered in garlic and thrown over a fire. A large piece of grill became essential as it was possible to cook three items in different saucepans at the same time, a difficult operation to attempt with one camping stove.

The tool kit shrank dramatically when we discovered that most of the ring spanners in our set did not fit any nut and bolt on either bike. The medical kit, currently large enough to equip a small hospital in the bush, was reduced to a more practical size. Personal wardrobes were also severely curtailed; I decided I could live without socks and was forced to part with the pair of Katharine Hamnett jeans which had cost me a small fortune only a month before. (It was particularly annoying when the equipment manager then insisted that we all bought a pair of jeans in Harare to look 'respectable'.)

As a large pile of discarded clothes and equipment amassed beside our tents, we discussed the plan for the following day. The front mountain bike wheel was cannibalised to make the trandem roadworthy, and it was agreed that one unfortunate person would have to hitch to Francistown. Some of the surplus equipment was too valuable to give away so this unfortunate person would have a lot to carry and the nightmare task of trying to sell it all. Dave, who came third in the 'North American Spoofing Championships', called for another game of spoof. Five minutes later Dave and I were staring nervously at each other and making our calls.

'Two,' Dave offered.

'Three,' came my hesitant reply.

We opened our hands to reveal a total of three; relieved, I watched Dave resign himself to the nightmare ahead.

The task of giving away the clothes fell to me. The following morning I wandered into the shop and presented them to a delighted *ma*. She ushered me towards a huge fridge and produced a whole fresh goat's liver, the prize part of a recently slaughtered animal. It was the first of many displays of the boundless generosity we were to experience throughout Africa. I felt embarrassed, but aware that the greatest offence would be to refuse it. I thanked her profusely and set about frying it with garlic and onions for breakfast. It was absolutely delicious and the massive protein boost led to some manic cycling; the three of us went on to cover eighty miles that day. We had left the equipment manager at the roadside, aptly obscured by the display of precious equipment and the mountain bike draped over his shoulder.

A roadsign marked the Tropic of Capricorn and we stopped under the shade of a large acacia for cold drinks and cigarettes. Having resisted temptation for the last four months I was surprised to find myself smoking two or three filterless French cigarettes every time we stopped. This gathered momentum – the more we cycled the more I smoked, giving my lungs absolutely no chance to purge themselves. Chris and Dave succumbed as well, leaving Steve as the only member of TMOAB really qualified to wear the yellow baseball caps, donated to us by one of our sponsors, Stoppers anti-smoking lozenges.

Some long gentle downhills provided respite from gradual inclines. The psychological battle with the kilometre posts was often more of a strain than the physical action of cycling – especially on this road which marked every half-kilometre, making it very difficult to escape a never-ending process of mental arithmetic, converting kilometres to miles and calculating estimated times of arrival at our current speed. Fortunately I managed to wean myself off this habit before driving myself completely insane. Cycling was still such a novelty and so physically demanding that mental processes were somewhat limited. No memorably earth-shattering thoughts at this stage, just putting one's head down and battling on to the next Coca-Cola.

After seventy miles I suddenly felt very weak. We were slogging slowly uphill, pulling our wretched caravan. Toppling off the saddle to fall asleep in the ditch beside the road was the most appealing thought I could muster. After eighty miles I found my second wind and we rolled into Mahalapye enthusiastically. Two white guys and their girlfriends had passed us earlier in a Toyota and now stood beside the road clapping as we drew alongside. We talked and they told us where to head for a cold beer and a large steak. We promptly found ourselves at the Mahalapye Hotel, a secluded old building with a small verandah covered in purple bougainvillea. Two cold beers each disappeared very quickly and with maximum effect, leading to another two, which in turn led to the suggestion of eating in the restaurant. We could afford a mixed grill each as long as we reached Francistown in two days. This did not seem a problem, so after pitching out tents and attempting to wash under an outside tap, we assembled in the small dining room. The mixed grill was rather disappointing but spirits were high and conversation animated. It was the first time I recall having a relatively personal conversation on the trip and offered a first glimpse of respective thoughts and feelings. Exhaustion soon overcame this vitality and we stumbled into sleeping bags.

A restless barking dog and my overactive mind denied me sleep, but thankfully our notorious 'early start' was delayed until nine. Once on the move we made good progress again, clocking up nearly eighty miles before dusk. We had just passed through the seething metropolis of Lachana – which must be the smallest village in the world to merit a roadsign of its own – consisting of a wooden hut and a jovial toothless old man anxious to inform us that 'dis place Lachana', when the buckled trailer wheel finally called it a day. We put on the spare, lethargically covered another few kilometres, and stopped to camp opposite a small gathering of corrugated iron shacks where we managed to find water. It was our first real night in the bush and on the road; the tremendous feeling of space remains vividly inscribed. Laurens Van der Post once wrote that 'every night you camp in the bush you leave a part of your self behind'. Even now I can recall that campsite in photographic detail: the low-lying scrub, a huge spider's web between two bushes, a mound shaped like Ayers Rock in the distance and a clear night sky turning turbulent and bringing rain. It was peaceful and prehistoric, untarnished by man.

The morning was dry and windy. We ate tinned sardines, drank huge mugs of tea and set our sights on Francistown, some ninety miles away. A puncture delayed us in the middle of the day and we pulled over by a garage with an adjoining food stall. Our remaining cash stretched to buying us our first bowls of *nsima*, the staple diet throughout sub-Saharan Africa. *Nsima*, or *ugali*, is a stodgy porridge made from maize-meal. It requires enormous effort to chew and digest, tastes like flavourless gum arabic and settles in your stomach like a block of cement. However many times I tried to convince myself that I liked it, even at a fever pitch of severe hunger, I repeatedly failed. The only redeeming feature about this lunch was being able to add some taste by squeezing a lime over it.

For the last twenty kilometres to Francistown we were tormented by large signs for the Marang Hotel, boasting about its swimming pool. While coasting downhill, savouring the idea of leaping into clear, cool water, there was a loud crack from the back of the bike. The dubious rubber tyre coupling had torn apart and we turned round to see the trailer somersaulting downhill towards us. On its first roll one of the angle-iron corners had dug a huge divot out of the tarmac, an indication of just how heavy this contraption was. This incident finally convinced me that trying to tow this burden any further than Francistown, let alone to Cairo, was our most foolish miscalculation to date. I immediately announced my intentions of throwing nearly everything away – a rash decision at this stage and one which prompted a short, heated exchange with Chris. A couple of minutes later we were talking sense again; we mended the coupling with another piece of car tyre and limped into Francistown, pausing every five minutes to pump air into a slow puncture.

Sweaty, tired and dirty we staggered into the Marang Hotel to find the equipment manager drinking beer and embroiled in an argument with a group of white South Africans. This was curtailed as we bombarded each other with respective problems and proposed solutions; confusion reigned and we retired to the campsite. Dave was somewhat surprised that we had all developed such severe hatred for the trailer, but soon realised that we were going no further pulling a caravan. He had managed to sell most of the stuff and had discovered 'punctureless inner tubes' – solid pieces of rubber. While TMOAB languished in disarray, the driver of the Toyota which had stopped for us earlier wandered across the campsite, introduced himself and extended an invitation to stay.

Peter B— was born in Kenya, educated at Cheltenham in England,

and now lived here running a small drilling business. He was a big, robust character with short black hair and a conventional appearance. He had served a few years in the British army and, judging by exploits recounted over the next few days, was an ex-SAS man. He had ridden a motorbike right through southern Sudan a few years earlier on his way south to Botswana, an impressive feat considering the lack of roads and the war in the area. He had built a wonderful thatched house on stilts, more or less with his bare hands, and a verandah looked out over a small but secluded garden. Giant bamboo and wood were used throughout and it was a totally functional and very comfortable house. He could not have been more helpful over the next few days as we arranged to send the trailer back to Gaborone and retrieve the faithful Pelican. The wire cage on the Pelican was immediately dispensed with, leaving room for the guitar to lie across the top, buffered by the two tents. Weight was distributed more practically, with only two sleeping bags and the blaster over the front wheel. The mountain bike became the pack horse, carrying four heavy panniers and all the tools.

While dealing with various jobs in town, Dave and I noticed posters advertising the 'One Stop Roots and Culture Night' at the New York Nightclub. That evening we made a perilous trip to town using a small torch to illuminate the path ahead, located the New York and left the trandem locked to some railings outside. There was little evidence of the 'One Stop Roots and Culture night' but a Zambian jazz band called the Broadway Quartet were about to appear on stage. We bought beers and settled into an alcove. The Broadway Quartet was quite brilliant and we stayed for the whole of both sets; the lanky lead singer did superb Louis Armstrong impersonations and the short retiring lead guitarist was clearly no beginner.

Word circulated to the manager about the trandem and what we were up to. He found us in the crowd and asked whether we would get on stage and make a short speech about what he called our mission; he would then pass the hat round for donations to charity. Before I registered what was going on, I found myself onstage with Dave and the trandem, burbling into a microphone about 'our mission'. To my surprise it was greeted with enthusiastic applause and we raised some thirty pounds for AMREF by passing the hat round. It was almost embarrassing how spontaneously generous people were, considering their income, and I felt sickened by the attitude of so many people in London who had grumbled about donating one pound on a sponsorship form.

The following day we hit the road again with our reduced load and fully functional bikes. The Zimbabwe border was within a hard day's ride but we decided to stretch it to two so that we could cross over at a convenient time of day. The landscape became more interesting, undulating pasture replacing the monotony of flat, dense scrubland. More acacias appeared, spreading their much appreciated shade and lending an East African savannah-feel to the landscape. At Tsheshebe, we alerted the chief to our presence and were shown to the village courtroom to camp for the night. We cooked large pieces of fillet coated in garlic, baked some sweet potatoes and, for the first time, it seemed normal and natural to be where we were. Clouds of sepia surrounded the full moon, shedding monochrome light over silent silver bush.

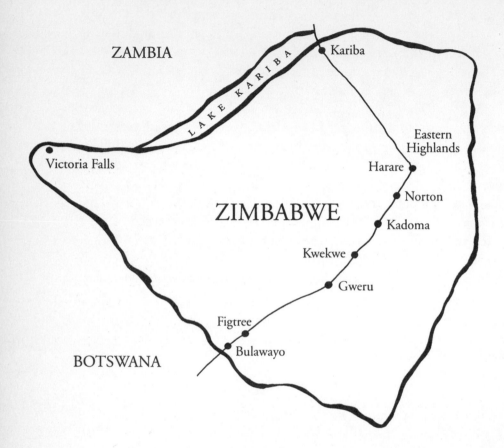

ZAMBIA

LAKE KARIBA

Kariba

Victoria Falls

ZIMBABWE

Eastern
Highlands

Harare

Norton

Kadoma

Kwekwe

Gweru

Figtree

Bulawayo

BOTSWANA

O – 500M
APPROX. SCALE

Zimbabwe

Border towns throughout Africa were invariably strange. A mixture of black-market hustlers and children selling boiled eggs and samosas drifted through the control barriers, in and out of no-man's-land, appearing to be of indeterminate origin. The bedraggled, crumbling town of Plumtree was no exception and it reminded me of the scene when Butch and Sundance arrive in Bolivia – quiet, depressed and apathetic.

The decaying colonial buildings housed empty shops and a hotel where the bar seemed to have monopolised any thriving business in town. Steve was tempted by some prehistoric pork pies behind the bar and we ordered four bottles of Zimbabwean beer. (Trying the local beer was to become a bit of a ritual whenever we entered a new country). We also inquired about some lunch. Twenty minutes later four soup bowls appeared but our expectant appetites suffered a severe jolt when confronted with the contents – a parboiled cow's hoof complete with hair and swimming in a thin greasy stock. For a few minutes I wrestled with the question of putting this lump of fat, bone and hair into my mouth and concluded that I was not quite that hungry. Meanwhile a party of eight at the next-door table were gnawing little scraps from their assorted selection of feet. We adjourned to the shops, bought four steaks for the price of a pair of hooves and assuaged our hunger.

By the next morning the pork pies had taken their toll on Steve's stomach and progress was postponed. The day was memorable only for the fact that Chris nearly caught a fish in the nearby dam. Never has 'the one that got away' been such an appropriate reference as Chris regaled us with stories about the supernatural size of this monster on the end of his line.

The following day was the first time that we managed to get lost. Having ambled our way over the forty kilometres to Figtree, we spent the middle of the day surrounded by flowering bougainvillea in the shaded garden of a hotel. The staff assured us that a dirt road to the right took us into the Matopos Game Reserve, famous for its white rhino, and that we could make our way from there to Bulawayo by nightfall. Eager to cycle through a game park and see some rhinos, we followed their advice. The dirt road was a struggle for the trandem and trailer, but we covered the sixteen kilometres in under an hour before hitting tarmac. For some reason we turned right onto the road which circuits the area, and over the next three hours we cycled some fifty kilometres in the wrong direction around Matopos Game Reserve without seeing a single rhino. The terrain in the golden haze of evening was typified by large boulders perched on top of small ridges, like giant natural sculptures. The sun was already down by the time we saw a sign post for the Matopos Sailing Club. It was the first sign of life for two hours so we careered in to ask for directions. Turning off the tarmac, we bumped our way down some gravel and drew up in front of a dozen geriatric whites sitting on a verandah drinking gin and tonics. Rather bemused by this sudden intrusion, they asked where we were going. It was too tempting in the circumstances not to reply 'Cairo', which clearly caused little amusement, as they continued to stare at us as if we were alien creatures. Gradually this air of tension subsided, and we asked if we might buy a beer. There was some complication about us not being members, but after some consultation we were accepted, much to the alarm of one red-faced old buffer who continued to scowl at us from his deck-chair.

I could hardly believe the road into Bulawayo – a wide stretch of dual carriageway, lined with large houses and immaculate colourful gardens, perfectly mown lawns and the cleanest streets that I have ever seen. The centre of town appeared as affluent as the suburbs suggested, a mixture of modern high-rise blocks and colonial style façades with verandahs and wrought-iron railings. It felt like a prosperous trading town in the wild west, the streets designed on a grid pattern and famed for being wide enough for an ox-wagon to turn round. The Goodloid continued to attract attention but we were spared being surrounded by large crowds. The campsite is set in an arboretum in the centre of town where beautiful grass lawns weave round fabulous fully grown trees.

The five hundred pounds' sponsorship from Chloride would not be available until we reached Harare. Consequently we needed to finance ourselves for the five-hundred-kilometre ride ahead of us. We arranged local newspaper, TV and radio coverage, and started to approach companies, telling them all they had to gain by giving us a thousand Zimbabwe dollars (three hundred pounds); basically we would wear their T-shirts on TV in return for a small amount of local currency. Coca-Cola, Schweppes and Kenning Motors were not convinced, but the National Blankets Company was. The Zimbabwe TV crew were asked to film outside its factory gates, where a ceremonious presentation of the cash would occur.

Our beards were quite pronounced by now but had become so familiar to us that we no longer really noticed them. Only after looking at the photographs on our return did we realise just how bizarre we must have looked as we forced our way into meetings with managing directors. I am surprised that anyone gave us the time of day, let alone any money.

Zimbabwe TV and radio appeared at the great ceremony and the camera-man started to activate ambitious plans to capture the shots he wanted. Confidently placing himself on the rear seat of the trandem, he instructed his poor sound-man to balance precariously on the trailer behind. We were then asked to go as fast as possible downhill and to ignore the terrified shouts from the sound-man who was a shaking shadow of his former self when we reached the bottom. Dave then seized this prime opportunity to show off in front of camera on the mountain bike, painting black rubber marks on the tarmac as he skidded around. The camera team must have presumed him to be a famous European stunt cyclist because he drew more attention than the trandem, or National Blankets, for the next ten minutes. The National Blankets executives were not perturbed, looking on and muttering their approval: 'Ah yes, this is very good.' The presentation of the cash was conducted with great care and attention to protocol, and by midday everybody was happy.

A thousand Zimbabwe dollars was enough to iron out mechanical problems, (including building a wheel), to allow us a gastronomic picnic in the campsite, a brief journey (which we hitched) up to Victoria Falls to celebrate Steve's birthday and to keep us fed until Harare.

The Zambezi was in full flood, sending more water over the Victoria Falls than had been seen for over a decade. As a result, the cloud of spray was even more impressive than normal but prevented one being able to see much. Permanent rainbows arched across what we could see of the gorge, which is bordered by lush tropical vegetation thriving on perpetual 'rain'. The transition from this rainforest to the arid bush behind is abrupt and uncanny. The famous 'sound of thunder' (the noise of the water down into the gorge) can be heard for miles, pounding along like a relentless freight train; I found this constant rumble reassuring rather than threatening and we spent many hours mesmerised by cascading water.

On the first night we wangled our way into one of the smart hotels to watch a local band called The Black Merchants. Our request for some Hendrix slightly disrupted their repertoire of slow dance numbers, but since our appearance had doubled their audience, they seemed happy to oblige, giving us a mellow rendition of 'Hey Joe'.

Steve's birthday lunch was celebrated with 'Peaking Duck' – a spit-roasted duck stuffed with local herbs. This led to an afternoon running around the Falls like demented children, much to the annoyance of American tourists trying to protect their video cameras from the engulfing spray. Straying from the path to get a closer view into the gorge, I found myself with Chris, wandering through long wet grass, and Steve treading tentatively with bare feet behind us.

'I wonder if there are any snakes here,' I said to Chris as we reached the lip of the gorge.

Almost immediately I saw a black snake coiled up and basking in the sun before us. I turned to make a sharp exit and saw Steve hopping around like a maniac, trying to retrace his steps in the long grass as fast as possible.

A few minutes later we were firmly planted on the terrace of the Victoria Falls Hotel, wrestling with the knowledge that we could only afford one beer each. Just before leaving England I had torn my last cheque from my cheque book and grabbed my cheque card, hopeful that in some crisis situation they might save the day. Arguing that it was Steve's birthday and that, being such a smart establishment, the Victoria Falls Hotel might be the one place to accept my cheque, I had little difficulty in persuading the others to agree. General managers, assistant managers and finance managers appeared. Nobody was prepared to authorise our request until the bank manager was spotted having lunch in the hotel. He asked to see the cheque and I fumbled through my money belt looking for it. What I produced were the tattered remnants of a cheque folded up into a one-inch square. As I unfolded it more rips developed until I handed over what looked like a piece of intricate origami. Scrawled across the back were some telephone numbers and a map I had drawn in Francistown and the front was partially obscured with an ink stain. Unbelievably I was allowed to cash up to fifty pounds and we booked our table for dinner that night.

Despite desperate attempts to dress up we were refused entry to the dining room. Instead we were directed to the buffet outside – as much as one could eat for twenty Zimbabwe dollars. This was a dangerous invitation to offer TMOAB. We went berserk, piling our plates high with steaks, ribs, chicken, pork chops and salads. It almost makes me ill to think about it now and I remember suffering severe indigestion as I lay down to sleep.

We moved camp the following day, away from the town to a peaceful clearing further upstream. Chris pursued his attempts at catching fish for our dinner, but without success. One evening he was joined by Dave, who succeeded in plucking a tiny minnow from the waters of the mighty Zambezi and the following day he sat back in disbelief as a local with a home-made rod caught several large catfish in half an hour.

The bar in Chinotimba, the local village, typified what was to become so familiar. A large open arena, cement floors, wooden benches, a distorted jukebox and lots of very drunk people. The 'African beer', *Chibuku*, is subsidised in Zimbabwe, a plastic four litre bucket costing little more than fifty pence. Seated in groups of four or five, the locals pass the bucket between them on a continuous rotor. Brewed from

sorghum or maize, it looks like pale brown porridge and tastes dis-
gusting. However, a large proportion of the population seem to drink
it voraciously because these bars are open and full throughout the day.
If subsidising *Chibuku* is Mugabe's way of dissipating any political
threat from the masses of unemployed, then it has worked quite well. At
Chinotimba we made friends with a Zulu called Eliot, a huge man who
spoke good English in a bellowing gregarious voice. He loved music
and enthused wildly as Steve played for nearly two hours.

The early morning sun filtered through shaded avenues as we cycled out
of Bulawayo. The tranquility of a waking town was shattered by the
sounds of Led Zeppelin, the trandem was running better than ever and
the equipment manager was as perky as usual. Cycling on the trandem
became increasingly analogous to rowing, due to the sense of balance
and rhythm we had developed. The road rolled across small hills,
allowing us to gather momentum on each descent before powering
up the next incline. Rowing terminology was adopted to synchronise
our bursts of energy – a call to 'build her up' at the bottom of a
descent would send us into the next hill at high speed, and a 'take
her home' would drive us up to the crest. On this stretch we found
ourselves cruising up hills in top gear and averaging over twenty miles
per hour.

The landscape turned to Australian outback; eucalyptus groves
sheltered colonial farms amidst endless expanses of long, dry grass.
After sixty-five kilometres we pulled over beside an old man seated on
a rock, presumably waiting for a lift.

'I had a dream about you last night,' he stammered.

Surprised by this sudden revelation, we tried to confirm what we
had just heard.

'Yes, yes – three men on one bicycle,' he insisted.

Judging by his shocked expression, he was telling the truth. Having
said 'how weird' quite a lot, we pointed to a dusty path behind.

'Is there a village down there?'

'Yes – there is village.'

'Is it a nice village?'

'Oh, it could be nice,' was his vague reply.

He still seemed to be getting a grip on himself as we set off to investigate this mysterious village that 'could be nice.' A left fork in the path led towards a line of eucalyptus and a colonial farmhouse with corrugated iron roofing and a verandah. A pick-up truck drew up behind us, driven by a burly white farmer. After brief introductions he pointed to a clearing beneath the eucalyptus for us to camp and offered us a beer after we had pitched our tents. It transpired that he and his family had seen us on TV the day before and they sat patiently as Dave poured forth his catalogue of stories.

Savannah grassland continued, dotted with acacias and shrubs at the roadside. There were quite a lot of cattle in evidence, but also large areas seemingly untouched. The town of Gweru was our target for the day. We were twenty kilometres short when a metallic orange BMW came screaming past us before breaking hard and swerving towards the verge. As we drew up alongside, a beaming, buzzing face, crowned with a fuzzy afro, leered out of the window.

'D'ya guys wanna smoke some dynamite?' was his opening line as he rifled through the glove-box.

Inexperienced in the smoking of dynamite, we were intrigued.

He claimed to run a gold mine near Gweru, which seemed moderately plausible, and he made unnecessary boasts about his salary. However, it was an entertaining break at the roadside, and he was the owner of some fine dynamite which ensured an effortless ride into Gweru, where we camped in the sports club and suffered the drunken rascist bravado of two white rugger teams drinking in the bar after a game.

The next day's ride took us to Kwekwe. Roadside vegetation was denser again and the landscape less arid; Gweru seemed to mark the transition. The hills were longer and higher now, but we still refused to get off and walk, insisting on fighting our way to the top in first gear, oblivious to the strain imposed on the bike. That evening Steve jammed with two local guitarists and I made recordings with the Pro Walkman. Chris and Dave got carried away in the bar, and suffered the consequences in the morning.

After an absurd breakfast of cheese squidged together with onion and tomato, we took to the road once more, Chris and Dave moaning and groaning about the condition of their heads. At lunchtime we paused in a lay-by and were treated to one of Chris and Steve's pasta dishes – a congealed lump of stodge in a pan which ensured that they did not cook again for several weeks. Another forty kilometres in the afternoon took us to Kadoma where we were approached by a white couple and their five children. They kindly invited us to stay and bravely subjected their washing machine to our obscenely filthy clothes.

A gradual uphill and a strong headwind prevented us reaching Harare the following day. Exhausted and hungry, we pulled up by a shop in Norton, ate all their steak pies and a bag of home-baked biscuits. Half an hour later we were all feeling ill, concluding that pies in Zimbabwe were something to be avoided. We were given a room in the Norton Hotel at a reduced rate and fought off incessant in-house calls from the resident girls offering their services.

The headwind was even more vicious in the morning and, together with the biggest hills so far, it made progress painfully slow, as we battled our way into Harare at midday. We went directly to the Chloride office where we collected mail, discovered that the spares package had not even left England and that the British High Commission had never heard of us, despite all our previous correspondence. Depressed by this news, we started to make plans. The spares package would take at least a week to arrive and clear customs. Staying in a city for that long would be too expensive and we badgered Dave to ring one of his 'contacts'. This he eventually did and moods changed dramatically when we heard that we had a place to stay and would be picked up that afternoon.

The tenuous contacts were Kenneth and Lesley S—. It transpired that they had met Dave's father once about twenty years ago. Lesley, a former Miss Rhodesia, was in her early forties; she had beautiful long red hair and high cheekbones. At four thirty she appeared outside the Chloride building in a pick-up; we loaded both bikes and the trailer, apologising for our extraordinary attire.

'Oh no, I think it's rather jolly,' she replied.

Blissfully unaware of what to expect, we found ourselves ten kilometres out of town, turning off the road into an avenue of tall cypresses.

The driveway extended for about two kilometres and led to an enormous pink villa, partly hidden by one huge eucalyptus. An atrium-style dining room opened onto the garden behind and a tower with a tiled roof reminded me of Tuscany. A secluded area behind a row of cypresses became our camp.

'Now, why don't you have showers in the house and get changed for dinner?' she offered, clearly assuming that we had other clothes to change into.

Too embarrassed to admit that we were already wearing the sum total of our clothes, we shuffled upstairs. Chris really had problems. His evening wear at the moment involved removing his shorts and retaining his boxers. The only solution was to chop and change what clothes we did have and reappear looking slightly different from before. I came clomping into their grand drawing room wearing what was once a white jersey, tucked into Steve's Empire Builder shorts, with Timberland boots on my feet, convinced that I looked respectable.

Kenneth turned out to be seventy, slightly deaf and recovering from a hip operation. He still referred to Zimbabwe as Rhodesia and Malawi as Nyasaland. Sitting in his white leather armchair, I had the impression that he was not particularly enamoured by our appearance. Chris, Dave and I had managed to humour him a bit when Steve entered the room, barefoot and wearing blue cotton karate trousers turned inside out to obscure the dirt. There was a slight pause while Kenneth regained his composure and the conversation about farming was resumed. Assuming that we were talking on a national rather than personal level, Steve interjected: 'Well, it's a matter of using their resources properly.'

Kenneth interpreted this as a criticism of his own farming methods and retaliated in an uproar.

'So you know do you?' he boomed.

Steve was off to a bad start. Kenneth also could not deal with the fact that someone could wear an earring and still be heterosexual, and Steve was branded a 'gay communist' from then on. Lesley, on the other hand, adored him, romanticising him as Keats and me as her Don Quixote – a source of much mirth for Chris and Dave. Both of them tried to display an open-minded attitude to Africa and her people but seemed unable to extricate themselves from an entrenched colonialism.

An extraordinary situation developed. Kenneth made his sentiments clear, dropping hints about filling in the visitors' book and camping at the end of his two-kilometre drive. But Lesley seemed keen for us to stay, driving us to appointments in town with ZBC and insisting on giving us mattresses to sleep on. She even tried to move two of us into the house. Quite soon it became evident that we had to go. The house had become out-of-bounds and we were careful to make ourselves as scarce as possible.

Chris's birthday was looming and we decided to celebrate in town and move on the following day. Riding into Harare with one feeble torch between us, we went in search of The Archipelago, a recommended nightclub. Once again we found ourselves very sober and very poor, the birthday allowance disappearing on a beer and a tequila each. Chris then produced a ten pound note from his money belt – worth up to sixty Zimbabwe dollars on the black market.

A seedy-looking white pimp was sitting nearby.

'If I can get fifty dollars from that guy then I'm allowed to spend it all on tequila,' I announced.

'OK,' was the unanimous verdict.

A minute later I had sixty dollars in my pocket and was heading for the bar. By five in the morning we were predictably deranged; Steve was being reprimanded for falling asleep while the rest of us were plied with free Scotch by the management and invited back gratis the following night. As I stumbled onto the street with the birthday boy, we were set upon, for no apparent reason, by six young coloured guys. Dave and Steve appeared from the club to find Chris and I lying in the road being kicked and an aggressive confrontation ensued, leaving Chris with two black eyes. In a subdued stupor we wound our way back, the crisp dawn air helping to alleviate the pain of multiple bruising.

The spares package arrived on the Monday morning but remained impounded in customs awaiting clearance. Taking advantage of this further delay, we spent a few days in the Eastern Highlands, a semi-mountainous area near the Mozambique border. For five pounds a night we rented a small chalet overlooking an artificial lake created by the Udu Dam. Long treks took us all over the surrounding area which, incongruously, felt Mediterranean as well as Scottish – yellow sandy soil and rocky outcrops clashing with moorland scrub. The hill facing the chalet looked over a lunar landscape beyond, an uninhabited wasteland shrouded in a dreamy bluish haze. An attempt to scale a near-vertical face of this hill had me burning the ends off my fingers as I slid thirty feet down the rock. From the summit Dave and I struck off towards the town a few kilometres away, inadvertently straying through the middle of a firing range before reaching the market, where we found piles of over-sized fruit and vegetables; one avocado fed the four of us for dinner.

Back at the chalet, we received startling news. Chris had caught two fish. From this moment on he was nicknamed Trout and our confidence in his fishing was renewed. We had to vacate our chalet the following day due to bookings from Harare and after two unbearably cold nights camping we returned to the capital.

Ralph Stutchbury is a film producer, born and raised in Zimbabwe. He lives with his girlfriend, Gerry Jackson, who hosts a rock show every Saturday afternoon on Radio Zimbabwe. I had spoken to him before leaving for the Eastern Highlands and now he extended an invitation for us to stay. They were incredibly hospitable, very laid back and an enormous help over the next few days.

Anxious to hear about the 16 mm film I had sent back, I rang London from Chloride and discovered that a fault with the camera had rendered ninety per cent of the material unusable. While I languished in terminal depression, Ralph suggested going to a camera repair specialist called Karl Kemp who, unbelievably, had done his apprenticeship for Bolex. I watched him dismantle the camera in seconds and, as predicted by our agent in London, we realised that the claw which pulls the film through the gate was not synchronised with the shutter, creating a jarring image.

Using specialised tools, Karl remedied the problem as we discussed the journey ahead. I left with renewed confidence about making the film, cycling fast through the suburbs.

The High Commission had helped extricate the spares from customs without our having to pay duty. A spare rear wheel with a specially fitted drum brake sent the equipment manager into pure ecstasy. It was immediately christened 'The Wonderful Wheel of Ninon' which, in respect of its performance, proved rather premature. For a start it arrived without wheel-nuts. The heavy-duty axle was oversized and had an unusually fine thread; it took two days of sifting through nuts and bolts in various garages and hardware shops to find ones that would fit. While we were riding back through Harare and rejoicing about our imminent departure, one of the pedals decided to drop off. The thread was completely stripped. According to welders in town there were two options: to build up the pedal arm thread and re-machine it, which would take two days, or in one day build up the stripped thread in the pedal crank with aluminium and then rebore it. Ralph suggested visiting a friend of his down the road and after a delicious curry we drove through the suburbs to his house. Nigel turned out to be an advertising executive and a vintage car fanatic – an immaculate Mk.II Jaguar was sitting next to a 1932 Lagonda in his garage. We showed him our problem and he remarked how similar the thread on the pedal was to a spark plug; some accurate measurements confirmed that it was almost exactly the same and he suggested a 'helicoil'. (Apparently this is a technique used quite often on VWs; the existing thread is bored out by a tool which leaves a new coil thread behind.) His advice proved sound and the next day our preparations were complete.

One crucial decision was still in the balance – whether to join the military convoy through Mozambique or head north to Zambia. Chris, Steve and I favoured Zambia. The convoy had been suffering a spate of attacks from Renamo guerrillas and, even if uneventful, this route would bring us into Malawi way ahead of schedule. Going through Zambia would mean cycling many more miles and consequently raising more money for charity. Theoretically we could stay on schedule and we discounted the bad stories about Zambia as pure exaggeration – if they were not, then it could hardly fail to be an interesting place to travel. Also Ralph had told us that Clint Eastwood was shooting *White Hunter*, *Black Heart* at Kariba, conveniently on our way to the Zambian border. Dave had no option – Zambia it was.

Our departure was inevitably delayed. The Wonderful Wheel of

Ninon, complete with wheel-nuts, now decided to tighten upon itself, making it difficult to achieve speeds of more than five miles per hour. Trying to set the locking nuts resulted in a tedious process of tightening two nuts together on one side to prevent movement, as trial and error determined the perfect setting on the other.

The sun had sunk to a suffused golden glow behind a line of eucalyptus as we cycled through the suburbs. Hendrix was screaming about 'Crosstown Traffic' and regenerated muscles were driving us along at high speed. A small blue car drew up alongside, driven by a grey-haired old woman. She started waving her hands towards the kerb and we pulled over.

'And where do you think you're going?' she asked.

'We're heading for Kariba.'

'But it's nearly dark – where will you stay tonight?'

'Oh, just somewhere in the bush.'

'What do you mean? You can't sleep in the bush – there's nothing there – follow me back to my house.'

She left no time for further questions and, feeling like awkward schoolboys, we did as we were told.

Olive Smith is eighty-five and lives with a faithful old maid called Judith. Considering our appearance, we were stunned that she almost forced us to come and stay. She had come to Africa with her husband on the first Flying Sunderland trip in 1948, landing on the Nile, Lake Victoria, Lake Tanganyika and the Zambezi. She spoke nostalgically about her early days in Rhodesia, plying us with cooking brandy after an enormous fry-up. (Olive did not drink, but doused all her meals in brandy, insisting that all the alcohol evaporated in cooking.) Cooking brandy combined with fatigue and we found ourselves falling asleep in front of episodes of *Bread*, sent over on video by her son in England.

Finding our way back through the suburbs the following morning proved quite hazardous. Seeing us pass, an oversized pitbull terrier came hurtling out of a driveway. Our sedate early morning cycle rapidly became a manic race as we tried to get away from this three-foot lump of barking, menacing muscle. Starting at the front, it leapt up to grab Dave's leg, but was thwarted by a Timberland boot thrust purposefully in its face. Having lost some ground, it tried for Chris in the middle, only to receive similar treatment. By the time it tried for me on the back, it was in a total frenzy, displaying large dribbling jaws and teeth that a shark would have been proud of. I stamped my right foot into the top of its head before finding the pedal and helping our escape. If able to keep up with us, it would have most certainly kept trying to bite our legs and I now regard it as one of the most threatening animal encounters of the year.

Puffs of cloud drifted slowly across a blue sky as we passed fields of ripening corn on a flat road. While listening to 'Strawberry Fields' and discussing the genius of The Beatles, the front wheel fell against the left fork and brought us to a standstill. Loosening the wheel-nuts revealed a crack in the cup which holds the axle. A short walk brought us to a garage where a big bearded man called Zebra set to work with his welder. Using a template, he cut two supporting brackets which he welded onto the forks above the axle cups. I shot two rolls of film, eager to capture what we had deemed to be a major crisis.

About a hundred kilometres north of Harare, beside the main road, near Chinoyi, there is a crater about a hundred feet wide and seventy feet deep. At the bottom a clear, translucent pool recedes into a tall, narrow cavern. A tunnel winds its way from the surface to a point about thirty metres above the water; lying on a slightly inclined ledge it is possible to look directly down. This first glimpse of the water left an indelible impression in my mind – an electric aquamarine blue, beaming with such an intense aura that I initially presumed ultra-violet lights had been installed. Rocky crags disappear into a seemingly bottomless abyss, visible to such depth and with such clarity that it seems unnatural. Looking from directly above, it was impossible to gauge where the water level was until we dropped a small stone. After it splashed we watched it falling, like an asteroid through space, for a further thirty seconds, until it was too small for the human eye to see. The pool is known to be at least three hundred and fifty metres deep but recently a German team trying to go deeper, disappeared without trace. Local legend claims that it runs underground to the sea and theories about its formation are inconsistent. The most logical explanation seems to be that a meteorite was responsible. However, it would have had to hit the earth at an unbelievable speed to have fallen over four hundred metres into the rock. There is little to explain why the water should be such an extraordinary colour; the crater is at an angle to the ground level and the pool is consequently shielded from the sky by overhanging rock. Whatever the theories and explanations, it is one of the most extraordinary natural phenomena I have ever seen. An eerie silence pervaded the place and the thought of swimming across the top, let alone diving down, was disturbing.

The following morning Dave made a solo expedition down the tunnel to what is signposted as the 'Wonder Hole', recording his impressions on the Pro Walkman. Comments like 'Wow – purple haze' were interrupted with high-pitched screeching as bats came diving from crevices above.

Almost every small town on Zimbabwe's main roads has a campsite equipped with barbeques, firewood and an ablutions block. For fifty pence each we could have access to these luxuries, so the day's journey would often be determined by the distance to the next campsite. We rarely cycled more than eighty kilometres a day at this stage but the hills and the heat made that enough to feel shattered in the evening. The long stretches of camping in the wild lay ahead of us so we exploited these perks while we could. It put a different perspective on our evening activities, often meaning that at least two of us would be lured to a local bar. Life was cheap and relatively easy for us in Zimbabwe; we were financially secure enough to afford beers, and supermarkets were comprehensively stocked with endless temptations. We would never have it so good again and we knew it. We sustained this lifestyle for six weeks and spent only three hundred pounds between us in that time, largely thanks to the thriving black market.

Saturday came and, with it, high expectations of Gerry's radio show. We tried to cover the eighty kilometres to Karoi in time to tune in at two but some high escarpments combined with the habitual breakdowns left us a few kilometres short when she came on air. Steve had to contend with the aerial sticking in his face as well as fiddling with the tuning on the front. To our surprise she mentioned us immediately, informing us that Chris's fishing reel, which he had left at their house, was now waiting for us at Kariba airport. She went on to describe the bike and the charities, asking anybody who saw us on the road to give us a friendly wave. At this point a lunatic driver screamed past, slammed on the brakes and pulled over under a tree ahead.

'Oh no, it's Dynamite again,' said Steve.

The driver proved to be even more nefarious than Dynamite, calling himself 'Tony Montana' and describing himself as 'a piano player – a bit of this and a bit of that', with arms outstretched and fingers splayed. He was Portuguese-Angolan, very affable, but as crooked as they come. He had found himself passing us just when Gerry mentioned us on the radio. Instead of a friendly wave he gave us a beer each and we sat down for a little session in the shade. After beers and a few smokes he raced off as fast as he had appeared.

Once in Karoi, we settled into the hotel garden and listened to Gerry play all our requests. Some Zeppelin, Joe Cocker, Hawkwind's 'Silver Machine' for Chris but, much to his disappointment, no Van for Steve. The campsite was on the edge of a reservoir and was spread over a series of terraced banks. The equipment manager excelled himself, constructing something he called a 'French Arrow', to cast hook and line into the water; it was an utterly useless device which plummeted into the lake about five yards away. The TMOAB board game, which had been developed in the Eastern Highlands, made another appearance; we had constructed a monopoly-style board with three levels, which corresponded to raising money in London for your expedition, gathering necessary equipment in Africa and completing a round of three threatening tasks – cycling across the Nubian Desert, through impenetrable jungle and up Kilimanjaro. Success in these three missions led you to 'a life of unbridled pleasure on the Planet Zoll'. Nobody ever got close to Planet Zoll and we concluded that it needed various adjustments before we sold it for millions to Waddingtons.

Karoi to Makuti took us over two fiendish escarpments. The poor Goodloid took the strain as we struggled up in first gear, tottering about at less than walking speed. At the crest of the second escarpment we were rewarded with the fastest downhill to date. Fast downhills on the Goodloid were exhilarating – they also stretched a sense of trust between us to the peak. The two passengers had to have complete faith in their driver to avoid the potholes they could see looming up ahead. Steering was the most exciting position because the sense of speed was so pronounced; however, a momentary lapse of concentration could have had terminal consequences. The weight of an eighty-kilo trailer and three people gave us incredible momentum, and sitting astride a vibrating 1930s frame felt very different from being solo on a modern mountain bike. The man up front had the added complication of watching the digital speedo, which was mounted on the right fork close to the hub, looking up and down to watch for potholes and shouting out the speeds as they flashed up; 'forty-two . . . forty-three . . . forty-four'. On this occasion we notched up forty-five miles per hour before levelling out and breathing again. The thought of a blow-out at these speeds, especially on the front, was never far away and this time I realised how lucky it was that the front fork had cracked a few days before and not now. The feeling of freedom at these speeds was euphoric and we enhanced this, when riding as passengers, by standing up on the pedals with arms stretched out to the sides – this approximated to physical flying more than anything I have ever known, gliding silently through the air at speed, a few feet above the ground and without the distraction of an engine beneath you.

The hotel disco in Makuti made sleep impossible until three in the morning. At five we were woken by loud South Africans packing their Land Rover for a safari into the nearby game reserve. Our fragmented sleep made for a disagreeable breakfast, during which we complained bitterly about paying so much to camp there – then received a full refund and profuse apologies from the manageress. Expectations about the day's ride had been running high since Harare. Without exception everybody told us to expect a lazy but potentially dangerous day, coasting downhill through the game park. The view towards the lake confirmed this, the road dropping into a large basin below us and disappearing into a carpet of scrub. We dismissed ideas of an early start, revelling in anticipation of the effortless day ahead.

During breakfast I noticed that my St Christophers had done their disappearing act again. Nervous about the ominous implications as we entered lion-infested territory, I started to panic. Seeing me grovelling around in the campsite, four staff from the hotel slouched over and asked what I was looking for. A farcical scene ensued as the five of us scrabbled about on all fours, turning every blade of grass. A ten-minute search revealed nothing so I raced back to the bikes and started unpacking the trailer. Unable to distinguish one from the other, I unpacked both tents and found the St Christophers nestling in a corner. Audible sighs of relief spread round the breakfast table.

Before we had even reached the beginning of the game park, eight hundred yards up the hill two bottom brackets had sheared. Struggling up hills in the last few days had clearly taken its toll. Fortunately we had spares and half an hour later we were roadworthy, dropping immediately into a long downhill curve. However, our visions of a constant descent were quickly shattered; a series of undulating ridges typified the whole stretch and some hills were comparable to the monster we had slogged up the day before. Our repertoire of in-jokes was expanded to encompass these latest pieces of misinformation.

'Oh, yes, all downhill to Kariba', and 'We'll be there in a couple of hours'.

When they did come, the downhills were fast and perilous. The trandem gathered momentum so fast that excessive braking was necessary to get round corners on the right side of the road; this in turn over-heated the wheel rims and caused punctures. As we dropped down lower, the temperature climbed higher. Needless to say we suffered the majority of punctures during the middle of the day – now referred to as 'the mad dog' (thanks to Noel Coward) – leaving each of us surreptitiously scanning the surrounding bush, careful not to be noticed by the others for fear of being branded paranoid.

After four hours of what was supposed to be a two-hour ride we had covered forty of the seventy kilometres. We had run out of water, replaced two bottom brackets and mended seven punctures. Severe thirst drove us to drinking the dodgiest water to date, provided by stagnant little pools covered with green algae. Several cars passed as we sat at the roadside with the trandem turned upside down. In view of the fact that we were immobilised in the middle of a game park, densely populated with lion, I was surprised that nobody stopped. In the afternoon somebody did – a friend of Chris's from England who had been working in Harare and was on his way back from having squandered his wages in casinos.

Four punctures later we arrived at Kariba airport, collected the fishing reel and drank several cokes each. The last stretch included the worst hills so far and when we finally reached the lake we were totally exhausted. Our two-hour sojourn through a game park had become an eight-hour nightmare with sixteen pit-stops.

A sign to the Kariba Breezes Hotel appeared at the top of a hill. Unfortunately it showed that the hotel was a kilometre away at the bottom of a steep road to the left; walking up it at this stage of the day would be very boring but we had to risk it in the hope of finding Clint. Unshaven, dishevelled and dirty, we presented ourselves to security at the barrier. At the same time a VW Combi drew up beside us, driven by a young German and his beautiful girlfriend. As he talked to us, we fought for a prime view through the window, transfixed by the sight of the girl. Recovering from shock, we discovered that they were employed as extras on the film and, if we were lucky, there might be more work available. Immediately we went in search of the casting director, and marched into the production office at the hotel.

The production team almost visibly recoiled when we walked through the door. The assistant director took a vehement dislike to the sight and smell of four vagrant hobos, proclaiming that no more extras were needed. The casting director, a white Zimbabwean from Bulawayo, was less dismissive.

'Give 'em a shave, a haircut and some clothes and they'll be right.'

'We'll see. Wait outside and we'll let you know.'

Half an hour later, Steve-the-diplomat was sent back in. He re-emerged with a glowing animated expression.

'We've all got jobs for a week,' he announced, 'and that production manager just did a whip round, gave me one hundred Zimbabwe dollars and told us to go and have a decent meal in the hotel.'

None of us could believe it. The combination of physical exhaustion and sudden elation created an unreal feeling. I had expected this year to be full of strange encounters and surreal incidents, but never had I visualised anything like this. Here we were riding the Goodloid through Africa and landing jobs in a Clint Eastwood film. It almost had 'gotten weird enough for me'. A celebratory beer divorced me even further from reality and all I could say for the rest of the evening was – 'I don't believe this – what's going on?'

We were given special permission to camp in the hotel grounds beside a big green tent, which served as the wardrobe department, and in front of two hotel rooms which were devoted to hair and make-up. At four we were woken for haircuts. One of the hairdressers was an attractive blonde South African called Janine, and we jostled for position in the queue to try and secure the attention of her scissors. Dave's face lit up when she beckoned him towards the chair. He must have failed to charm her one bit because she gave him the most savage short back and sides imaginable, much to our assembled amusement. Chris, Steve and I were given more lenient 1950s styles before being shown to the wardrobe department. Dave was made to look even more ridiculous with a pork-pie panama hat perched on his head, a 'kipper' schoolboy tie, cotton flares that were too short and brown brogues. Chris and I disappeared inside voluminous thick flannel suits, while Steve escaped with an open-necked shirt and tweed jacket. By the time we arrived on set at Kariba airport, we were unrecognisable. Other extras, who earlier that morning had refused to acknowledge our existence, now seemed to regard us as respectable young gentlemen and deigned to talk to us. One woman refused to believe that we were the same people who had been shuffling around earlier in filthy, torn clothes, sporting long hair and silly beards.

As we crammed as much breakfast as possible into our mouths, Clint slouched into the hangar, his head trailing behind his shoulders. While checking out 'the Big C', the first shot was called and we made our way across the tarmac to an old DC-3. Steve and I had landed parts as passengers on the plane, and Dave and Chris milled in the crowd of waiting relatives at the airport. I found myself sitting by the aisle with Clint standing beside me. Action was called and we walked out onto the tarmac, racing along to try and keep in shot. Overacting to the hilt, Dave came storming out of the crowd towards us, forcing Clint and his entourage to veer off to the left. He insisted on doing this in every take and I felt sure we would be reprimanded for ruining precious film. They were happy with the shot by the time lunch was called and we followed the crowd towards two vast marquees, where First Unit Caterers from Chertsey in Surrey, had lunch prepared for a hundred and fifty people. There were roasts, fish, steaks and grilled kebabs; there was a table covered with every type of salad ever invented, mussels, exotic fruit and French cheeses. Needless to say we had a field-day, sitting down with pyramids of everything piled high on tiny plates.

We worked for five days and were paid thirty Zimbabwe dollars (ten pounds) each at the end of every day. Our next cycle would take us across the Kariba Dam and into Zambia so a general policy of squandering our wages each evening was adopted by all. A luxury hotel nearby housed a casino and was the focus for most of the film crew every evening. On our last night we joined the two assistant directors at the bar; a continuous stream of Zimbabwean tequilas appeared, followed by tumblers of some evil concoction incorporating rum, vodka and whisky. Within the hour the equipment manager was slumped over a Space Invaders machine, impervious to the electronic explosions in his ear. Both hotels were within the confines of the game park and it was quite common to see elephants gathered outside reception; at one a.m. Dave was woken by a hotel guard after an elephant had started to express interest in the amusement arcade and was hovering behind him. Meanwhile Steve and I had won a hundred and twenty Zimbabwe dollars at the roulette table and I was trying to convince him, 'put it all on red, mate.' Wisely he refrained from this but made the mistake of letting me play blackjack after I announced that 'I won eighty quid once'. It did not take me long to lose everything, concentrating harder on securing a position next to Clint than on the cards. It turned into a long night and at five we crawled back into our tents. At about eight I woke with the most shattering hangover of my life; I would love to know what goes into Zimbabwean tequila. The sun was already quite high and the tent was creating a greenhouse effect, making me sweat horribly. I crawled over to the shade of a nearby wall and resumed my sleep. An hour later I was woken by a guard prodding me with his truncheon. I opened my eyes to see the cavernous black nostrils of an elephant's trunk swinging inches above my face, about to suck my nose off. Whether this shock made my condition even worse I do not know, but for the rest of the day I could hardly move, speak, eat or drink. Departure for Zambia was delayed while I struggled to purge my system of toxic tequila, vowing never to touch the stuff again.

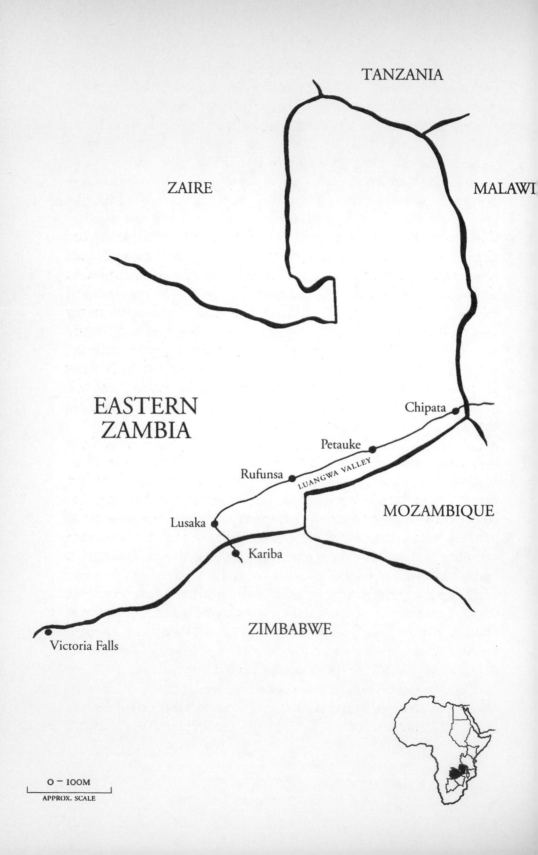

TANZANIA

ZAIRE

MALAWI

EASTERN
ZAMBIA

Chipata

Petauke

Rufunsa   LUANGWA VALLEY

MOZAMBIQUE

Lusaka

Kariba

ZIMBABWE

Victoria Falls

O — 100M
APPROX. SCALE

Zambia

The transition from the luxurious hotel environment of casinos and Clint Eastwood films, to a neglected corner of rural Zambia, could not have been more pronounced. Smooth modern asphalt turned to ancient potholed tarmac as soon as we crossed the Kariba Dam and were immediately presented with a long steep hill. Dave's new theory was that the trailer should be pulled up any hills by the mountain bike in a bid to lessen the pressure on the trandem. A few minutes later I was left grinding uphill, standing on the pedals to initiate any forward motion, cursing Dave and turning into a sweating beetroot. On reaching the border post at the top of the hill I made it very plain that I was *never* doing that again.

Poor Zambia had been given such bad press by people throughout Botswana and Zimbabwe that we had developed an image of an anarchistic nightmare. We were told that it was impossible to buy food anywhere and heard endless stories about people being shot at. Visions of being extremely hungry and under constant terror of bandit attacks could not have been further from our minds as we rode through quiet green bush, surrounded by butterflies. It was another beautiful day.

Two passing policemen stopped us, purely out of curiosity, informing us that we had arrived on a bank holiday weekend and that the banks would be closed for three days. Since there had been no bank at the border we were slightly bemused as to how we were to lay our hands legally on any Zambian currency.

'There's no food to buy anyway,' we joked.

A sign to the Manchinchi Lodge beckoned us off the road down a gravel track for two miles in search of somebody willing to change money on the black market. After accosting various people around the hotel, we changed five pounds with two girls reclining by the pool and immediately spent it all on beer and toasted sandwiches. Seeing an amplifier and speaker behind the bar, someone then had the bright idea of Steve singing for our supper. Realising that the time had come for him to justify the guitar's position on the back of the bike, Steve set out for the manager's office.

Gingerly popping his head round the door, he found the manager having tea with his family and launched into his embarrassed spiel about the Goodies' trandem, banks being closed, not having any food but having a guitar. Much to our surprise, Steve the Diplomat came back to the pool having been given vouchers for four dinners in the restaurant and a case of beer from the bar.

Swimming in the lake that afternoon was curtailed by the appearance of four-foot aquatic lizards.

That night, I appointed myself as Steve's manager and roadie, setting up the microphone stand, amplifier and speakers in the indoor bar. Steve tuned up and the rest of us started propping up the bar with two very drunk Zambian businessmen who, along with the barman, constituted the entire audience. At various stages of the '*gig*' I heard the crashing sound of breaking glass and kept looking behind the bar expecting to see a pile of broken bottles. Only after three songs did I realise that Steve was bashing the neck of the guitar against the stainless steel microphone stand to create his glass-breaking accompaniment. Bloated by beer and food, we braved local lion paranoia, walked across the peninsula and went to sleep. For weeks I had been musing, 'Maybe I'll sleep outside tonight'; finally the time had come.

The following morning Dave reminded us that he had 'come third in the North American Spoofing Championships', lost another game of spoof and was dispatched several miles in the wrong direction to buy food. We walked the trandem up to the main road, waited for Dave to come charging back, and set our sights on Lusaka. We had covered two miles when we noticed that the freewheel was dismantling itself, leaving a little trail of ball bearings in our wake. Things were starting to go wrong. The hills got steeper, the roads were the worst to date, temperatures soared and the trandem was far from happy. During one roadside maintenance session, the British Consul and his wife drove past in a Land Rover, on their way back to Lusaka after the bank holiday. Having been alerted to our arrival by the unintelligible brochures we had sent to every consulate along the route, he pulled over for a few minutes before continuing with our trailer crammed into his boot.

A purple haze hovered in dusty evening light as we pulled over by a small village looking for somewhere to camp. An area in the middle of some huts was cleared and swept by small boys using brushes made from twigs, and we were beckoned to sit down on low wooden stools. As a fire materialised before us, the village headman appeared, the fat stub of a large rolled cigarette sticking to his bottom lip.

'Here, smoke this one,' he said, thrusting the smouldering end towards us. 'This one, too much power . . . here . . . too much power . . . this one.'

It seemed important to experience the one-of-too-much-power and the headman joined us round the fire, accompanied by half the population of the village. One young man seemed keen to sell us a chicken and, after some mild bartering, Chris was volunteered to use his filleting knife on the ancient cockerel we were presented with. As we lapsed into the throes of the one-of-too-much-power, and pieces of chicken cooked over the fire, one man asked if we would like to try some of their food. Keen to sample some local delicacies, I accepted with zealous enthusiasm, oblivious to the enamel bowl which had been placed at my feet.

'Look at what you're getting to try man!' Steve pointed at the ground between my feet. I looked down to see a bowl full of furry, grey mice.

'I see what you mean,' I replied slowly, my enthusiasm waning.

At first I thought that they were fooling about, and this was some sort of joke to play on people under the influence of the one-of-too-much-power. Then one man plucked a mouse from the bowl, peeled back the fur on the belly and sucked out the entrails. He proceeded to eat the little legs, the tail and all the fur. We watched in astonishment as everybody else tucked into boiled mouse for dinner.

Later we discovered that the bush fires we had seen along the valley were lit to drive rodents out from the undergrowth. The rains had not reached the area in the last two years, crops had failed and these people had little, or nothing else, to eat.

Unfortunately our lightened load did not stem the systematic destruction of two freewheels the following morning and it was not long before a game of spoof was called to send one person ahead to Lusaka with the cannibalised mountain bike. Dave now refused to participate, having lost the day before, and a few minutes later Steve was hopping into a white Range Rover belonging to a mad Scottish aid worker called Dave. Within minutes the trandem was immobilised again and we started to walk the remaining sixty-five miles to Lusaka. After several miles, pushing the trandem up long escarpments in ferocious heat, we stopped beside the road for a meal. The sum total of our food supplies proved to be three onions, which we bit into like apples, and a tin of baked beans. We had no water and there had been no sign of any habitation for miles. A combination of these ominous factors led to us hitching a lift on a petrol tanker, arriving at the British Embassy to find Steve the Diplomat in consultation with Jeremy Legge, my sister-in-law's cousin, who was halfway through a two-year posting in Lusaka and kindly extended an invitation to come and stay with him and his wife Melanie.

Precautions taken to fortify houses in African cities are regarded as mandatory – barbed wire on high fences, broken glass embedded into the top of walls, massive chained gates and large, menacing guard dogs. Jeremy and Melanie's house was no exception. We camped in their garden for a few days, putting the necessary wheels in motion to get back on the road as quickly as possible and race towards Lake Malawi. Little did we know that our spares were not to arrive for another four weeks.

We moved from Jeremy's to stay with Ian, a VSO worker with a large, empty house and a big garden. Endless hours of reading every book he had in the house, right through to a *Medical History of Mental Disorders*, were occasionally broken up by the arrival of the local ex-pat brigade, who would sit out on the lawn drinking cold Irish coffee, shooting at chickens with their revolvers.

One night we offered to take Ian out to dinner and headed off to a restaurant-nightclub on the outskirts of town. Towards the end of our meal I spotted Tony Montana, 'the piano player', weaving through the crowd with two dodgy-looking sidekicks. We waved him over and were invited outside to the car park to meet his friends and have a smoke. His friends were all wearing black, standing beside black BMWs, dancing lethargically to heavy dub blasting from car stereos and smoking lots of strong grass. Tony disappeared for a few minutes in a BMW, only to return minutes later in a Mercedes. Men with AK-47s and walkie-talkies were wandering around the periphery of the car park. Something very dodgy was going on but we were not sure what. Later we discovered that Mandrax smugglers operate between South Africa and Tanzania, getting a new German car for every successful run.

Dave's family used to have an import-export business with an office based in Lusaka. When independence came, the company assets were frozen and Dave now started trying to prise the equivalent of twelve thousand pounds from the clutches of the Bank of Zambia. After umpteen visits to various banks over a period of weeks, some money was finally released. However, due to inflation and obsolete exchange rates used in the conversion, the Bank of Zambia had somehow managed to whittle twelve thousand pounds down to the equivalent of two hundred pounds in Zambian *kwatcha*. Having finally extricated this money, Dave now set off to spend some by taking us out to a dinner which, in 'real' terms, cost his father three thousand pounds. A packet of French cigarettes from the bar cost seven hundred pounds. Since the alternative was for the hard currency to remain at the disposal of the Bank of Zambia, this absurd extravagance almost seemed acceptable.

The chaos of the Zambian economy continued incessantly throughout our stay. The currency had been devalued by sixty per cent the day we arrived. Prices were decontrolled and then recontrolled every other day. Then it was announced that the currency was to be changed completely; everybody had two weeks in which to get to a bank and change their old *kwatcha* notes for new ones. The borders were closed for two weeks and riots broke out in all the big cities as people queued for days to get into a bank. In Lusaka they even ran out of new notes and people had to come back and queue again as they printed up more. I was always staggered to find that KK – Kenneth Kaunda – still enjoyed considerable popularity, despite the fact that the country had been in economic turmoil for twenty years.

I was equally dismayed to find that, despite having lost one son to the disease already, KK's government efforts to educate the people about HIV and AIDS were absolutely deplorable. Throughout our time in Zambia I did not see a single sign, advertisement or leaflet about the epidemic which was already killing thousands, except a little drawing of a pencil-thin man on a poster hanging in Immigration, which read 'AIDS *CAN* KILL'; nothing to tell you what the symptoms were, how you contracted HIV or how you could protect yourself from it. Talking to Zambians made me even more worried for their future; the few who did know that wearing condoms was a good idea did not seem interested in doing so; AIDS was just another killer disease to add to the long list that already existed.

Although the corruption and chaos of Lusaka was disturbing, Zambia started to grow on us. Apart from having money stolen by Jeremy's gardener, and somebody helping himself to my bananas as I walked down a street, we encountered warmth and generosity everywhere, from women selling vegetables in the market, to security men outside banks; a gentle strength of will which transcended the difficulties of life and kept everybody smiling.

Amongst the ex-pat community, we were, as usual, regarded with a mixture of disdain, bemusement and utter incredulity, but treated very hospitably. The Bush family were particularly long-suffering with us, letting us stay one weekend at their house in Siavonga, where we ate dinner at the bottom of their empty swimming pool. Tanvi, their daughter, became our friend and chauffeur in Lusaka, taking us down to the Oasis bar at night to drink weak, gaseous beer.

We were invited to one drinks party at a large colonial residence, where we met two attractive Italian sisters, one of whom was about to celebrate her twenty-first birthday. Through some circuitous route we were invited to attend her party – it was fancy dress, restricted only to the head and shoulders. Three Men on a Bike had no intention of complying to such limitations, so we set about decorating ourselves. With a *kakoi** twisted into a turban, a curly, painted moustache and Chris's absurdly baggy pants, I just about passed as Ali Baba. Dave had purloined, from the clothes market, a pair of genuine Seventies Brutus jeans, complete with twenty-eight-inch flares and latticework belt loops; combined with his floral Stephen King shirt, flowers in his hat and thick sideburns, he looked like a refugee from Woodstock. Steve resembled some eccentric colonial explorer in the ubiquitous Empire Builder shorts topped with a pith helmet and a David Niven moustache. Meanwhile Chris had painted his face black, green and brown and looked like a deranged Vietnam veteran on acid.

Predictably we were the last to leave the party, except for a large Dutchman, the managing director of Philips Electrical in Zambia who Dave had been drinking whisky with for most of the night. It transpired that Dave's grandfather, a famous oarsman, had been this man's hero, and he was so impressed with Three Men on a Bike that he wanted us all to go white-water rafting at Victoria Falls. The following day we went to see him at work. After a long tour of the factory and warehouse, we were seated in his office drinking beer, our discussion covering everything except white-water rafting, until combined pressure from the rest of us forced Dave to say:

'I don't know if you remember, but the other night you very kindly offered . . .'

'Oh no, I haven't forgotten. How much do you think you need?'

'Well, we worked out that if we take the bus down there and camp we can probably do it for six thousand *kwatcha*.'

'Six thousand doesn't sound like very much – here, take twelve and have a few beers while you're down there.'

---

* a piece of material about two metres long and one metre wide, worn around the waist like an Indonesian *sarong* or an Indian *lunggi*.

By offering to pay for her rafting trip, Tanvi persuaded her parents to lend us their Peugeot Estate. Will R—, an English guy in his thirties setting up a hotel on a plot of land upstream from Victoria Falls, offered us the option to stay at the tented camp on the site, beautifully positioned on a long bend in the Zambezi. We arrived to see an orange sun fade from an azure sky as hippos wallowed in the river below.

Lying down to sleep that night, on camp beds in a large tent, we were all quite alarmed by the proximity of so many large animals. Hearing something rustling in the tent made us all sit bolt-upright in our sleeping bags. The noise persisted and, since I was the closest, I was volunteered by everybody else to investigate. Clutching Dave's torch, I tiptoed my way towards the corner of the tent.

'It seems to be coming from this cardboard box,' I said nervously.

'Well go on then, open it,' Chris replied, impatiently.

All eyes were on me now as I closed in on the box. I flicked open the lid and jumped backwards. Peering in with the torch, expecting to find a large, venomous snake, I was relieved to find the cause of our combined terror – a tiny mouse, about two inches long.

The rafting was run by a group of American macho-surfie-types, based at one of the big hotels. The day trip is supposed to be paid for in hard currency, so our large brown paper envelope full of grubby old *kwatcha* notes did not go down too well. They relented after five minutes of Dave haranguing them about sponsored trandem expeditions and the Managing Director of Philips Electrical. Amongst the group assembling for the day were three mentally disturbed Italian geriatrics. They refused to accept that thundering down twenty turbulent rapids in a little rubber boat was beyond them. The Americans tried to explain that young people find even the walk down to the water at the start of the day difficult, let alone the raging torrents and the trek back up at the end of the day. The old man, who walked with a stick, was not put off, as he stumbled his way into the bus with his two chattering female accomplices.

At the top of the first near-vertical stretch of the path down to the river, the Italians reconsidered their options. After several minutes of rapid-fire conversation and wired gesticulations, they scrabbled and chattered their way back to the bus. Meanwhile TMOAB were racing down the edge of the canyon, led by Dave, who was bouncing from rock to rock like a downhill slalom skier, determined to be the first down. Assembled in our boat, with our Incredible Hulk skipper Mark, we set off down the rapids past basking crocodiles. Two unfortunate French women had been lumped in the same group and tried desperately to cling to a rope at the back as TMOAB leapt around the boat following orders from the Incredible Hulk, seated in the middle with two stabilising paddles. Adrenalin hit high levels as we were catapulted from rapid to whirlpool and propelled down the river like a spinning top. When the rapids levelled out further downstream I tried to envisage what would have been left of the Italian contingent.

Back in Lusaka we had news that the spares package had arrived. Pausing to leave a bottle of vodka with Jeremy and Melanie, we set off on a cloudless morning. As we left the outskirts of town a truckload of Zambian soldiers steamed past singing 'Goodie, Goodie, Yum, Yum'. Lots of cigarettes and gaseous beer now took its toll, causing me to reel around the market in Chongwe when we stopped for lunch. Local specialities on offer included charred black mice and small shrivelled quail-like birds. Feeling stronger in the afternoon, we started pushing ourselves harder. I remember the sensation of my frame seeming to noticeably expand as we cycled and seeing muscles appear in my thighs which I had never known existed. I was now two stone heavier than I had been when we set off from Gaborone three months previously. As the light softened we stopped at a roadside bar for a beer. A Norwegian voluntary worker drove up in a Land Cruiser and told us about hot sulphur springs a mile down the road.

A small pool, circled by tall rushes, sat steaming beside the road. The water was soft, pure and hot – so hot that it took several minutes to slowly immerse our aching limbs. A group of children sang beside the pool as the sun sank behind an escarpment, creating changing patterns of light in the rising steam.

In the morning I was woken by Dave, currently known as Dick McManic, splashing around euphorically in the pool. Revitalised after a cold night by the hot waters, we continued through the Unduanda region towards Rufunsa, where we stopped for lunch. Banana trees issued from hard, sun-drenched terracotta earth between circular mud huts with conical roofs. While cooking spagetti à la TMOAB and enjoying the one-with-too-much-power, the local guitarist came wandering through the banana plantation. His guitar had been cobbled together from an old petrol can, a wooden plank and some nylon fishing line. Weirdly enough he was tuned to exactly the same pitch as Steve and an impromptu jam broke out.

We hit forty-eight miles per hour that afternoon. Our streamlining tactics improved with time but forty-eight was not to be beaten for some months.

The following day we began a long and arduous ascent to the peak of Luangwa Valley. Spectacular views back to receding blue mountain ridges helped alleviate the monotony of pulling the trailer by hand. Levelling out onto a small plateau, we drew up beside a few huts to be greeted by a toothless old man asking if we had come to take a shower. Unaware of there being any showers in the area we shook our heads. He then pointed down a small path heading through the undergrowth on the other side of the road. Fifty yards down we found a cascading stream spilling into a small series of pools, broken up by smooth black boulders. Lush vegetation hung from above and the afternoon sun splayed through the trees. It was idyllic. Dave and I took it in turns to plunge our heads inside a small whirlpool, cleansing the mind.

Fine views of the surrounding valleys on our descent to the river were marred by the appearance of a long split in the rear tyre. Paranoia set in as we hurtled towards the valley floor, just managing to stop at a road block on the bridge. A tedious man in dark sunglasses insisted on scrutinising every page of our passports so we adjourned for drinks at the roadside. Steve's knee was starting to give him grief and after a two-mile walk up the far side of the valley, we collapsed beside the road, too exhausted to even cook a meal.

The following day we entered the tsetse fly zone. These infamous creatures are about the size of a horsefly and have a bite like an injection. They have the aggravating ability to land on your skin unnoticed, leaving their painful calling card before you have time

to swipe them away, and they seem drawn to moving targets. Three
bare backs on a bike consequently proved to be appetising prey. The
two front men on the trandem enjoyed the luxury of having the man
behind swat the little beasts as soon as they landed, while the man on
the mountain bike had to grin and bear it as he ground into another
incline. Trying to rest his swelling knee, Steve had elected to spend
all day on the mountain bike, something he soon regretted.

Distances and time during this stretch became distorted. Villages
marked as being thirty miles away on the map would suddenly
appear, and hotels promising refreshments in two miles would
take hours to reach. The Kachalola Motel was a prime example
as we struggled to leave the tsetse flies in our wake. Every passer-by
assured us it was 'very near' but it never was. Finally we stumbled
into the hotel, cursing tsetse flies, and ordered large amounts of food
to restore our spirits. Our progress that afternoon was curtailed by
bloated stomachs and the demise of Steve's knee. We camped on
sand in a small clearing, joined by a local poacher who took great
delight in showing us his weapon, a home-made musket which fired
large lumps of lead at unfortunate elephants. A strong wind blew up,
which, combined with the white sand, made me think of beaches and
the crystal-clear waters of Lake Malawi, beckoning like some distant
paradise.

Steve's knee had swollen so badly that there was no option but
for him to hitch ahead to Lilongwe with the mountain bike. We
left him beside the road, clutching his guitar in true hobo style, and
set our sights on Malawi. Swopping seats every ten miles proved
pyschologically more rewarding and we made fast progress in short
bursts. The hobo shot past us in the late morning, waving from the
back of a pick-up, but we caught up with him again at Petauke
petrol station where he was waiting for another lift. Cups of sweet
tea, Coca-Colas, huge meals and free *zolls* kept us ploughing on at
unprecedented speeds, only to be thwarted by an onslaught of sixteen
punctures over the next few days – all of them on the rim side of the
tube and all exactly the same sort of hole. We checked the tyres and
rims repeatedly but found nothing. Two weeks later we discovered
that the plastic layer of Tuffy Tape, which was placed between the

tyre and the tube to prevent punctures, was actually causing them by creasing the rubber.

Malawi had always beckoned like a promised land. The closer we came, the more appealing it seemed and the cycling took on a manic urgency reminiscent of Botswana. I found myself naturally hallucinating after about seventy miles and getting a second wind after eighty. The psychological battle with the mileage definitely did weird things to the mind and was impossible to escape from; the vision of the next ten-mile changeover and the possibility of tea and cigarettes, provided the mental propulsion that was often more of a challenge than the physical. The landscape had levelled out now and some of the road surface was beautifully smooth, creating a satisfying hum in contact with the tyres. The rocky burnt bushland of the Luangwa Valley had turned to sub-tropical savannah, and banana trees and palms replaced much denser vegetation.

The second day after leaving Steve, following a manic ride through 'the mad dog', we pulled over onto a dirt track advertising the 'Moonlight Bar – Now Fully Open'. As we veered off the road we hit a huge bump, tried to change down a couple of gears and ended up with the chain firmly lodged between the freewheel and the spokes. While we were frantically sticking screwdrivers into this carnage, an old man mellowed up and informed us that the Moonlight Bar was actually fully closed but would we like to have tea in his house across the road? This invitation was particularly memorable because of the chance to wash in a pool created by a dam in the nearby stream – complete immersion in water after sixty miles of cycling was invigorating and we returned refreshed to his house for tea. The small mud cottage was covered in purple bougainvillea; it was set apart from any village and was totally peaceful. He sat back in his wooden armchair and listened intently and with disbelief as we talked about our trip. He spoke excellent English and exuded a youthful innocence as well as the serenity of old age; we sat enthralled by another chance meeting.

Punctures were delaying us so much on the last leg to Chipata that we resorted to our spare rear wheel, the Wonderful Wheel of Ninon. This hub refused to run freely, seeming to tighten upon itself and

making progress painfully slow. By the time we ground into Chipata
we had reached a threshold of frustration; this was compounded
by the lack of Coca-Cola in town and bad vibes we received from
everybody we talked to. We tried to cure the rear wheel problem
by taking it to pieces in a garage vice, spent our last *kwatcha* on a
beer each and headed towards the border on a stretch of undulating
road. We stopped for the night by a small settlement of huts, cooked
an unusually horrible meal and took the rear hub apart again, this
time using an antique carpentry clamp provided by the enthusiastic
headman.

The promised land proved to be further than expected and we
arrived at the border with no local currency and no food in our
stomachs. Our hunger was prolonged by the Malawi border guards
who insisted on having a two-hour meeting when we arrived. Long
hair is against the law in Malawi, as are flared trousers – President
Banda's attempt at dissuading an influx of hippies. Hair seemed to
be growing at an unprecendented rate since our ordeal with Clint's
wardrobe department – so caps were worn throughout. Eventually
we ate at a small shack in Mchinji market, after changing a traveller's
cheque with the District Commissioner, and were quick to discover
the delights of Malawi – Choco-Mint biscuits and the staggeringly
cheap Tom-Tom cigarettes (paper packets of ten hideously strong
filterless cigarettes for three pence. The paper packet tends to fall
apart completely after the first cigarette, whereupon most of the
tobacco falls out of the remainder, leaving a serious mess in your
pocket). Although the availability of goods in the shops was in a
different league from Zambia, the people seemed even poorer, most
of the children wearing tattered rags over their distended bellies. The
market, however, was colourful and cheerful and the trandem started
attracting some of its biggest crowds to date while we ate mounds of
scrambled egg and hunks of fresh white bread. Hopes of reaching
Lilongwe that day had vaporised with the delay at the border; we
decided to take it easy, relieved to be in Malawi at last.

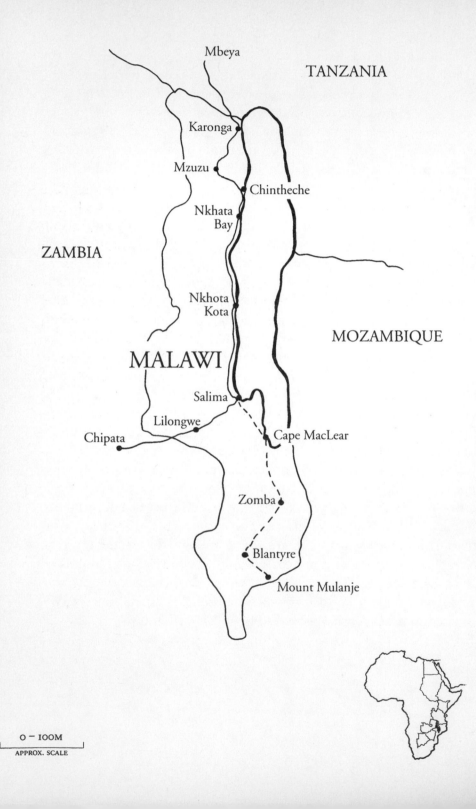

TANZANIA

Mbeya

Karonga

Mzuzu

Chintheche

Nkhata
Bay

ZAMBIA

Nkhota
Kota

MOZAMBIQUE

MALAWI

Salima

Lilongwe

Chipata

Cape MacLear

Zomba

Blantyre

Mount Mulanje

O — 100M
APPROX. SCALE

Malawi

Long-awaited Lilongwe persisted in being elusive. A strong headwind sent shivers through tall poplars as we approached the cardboard capital of Malawi, immediately finding our way to a hotel and bottles of locally brewed Carlsberg. Since Carlsberg markets three different beers in Malawi, our ritual tasting was extended. While comparing notes we were approached by John Carson, the Chloride MD in Malawi who had spotted the trandem outside the hotel lobby. He seemed even more excited than we were to have finally reached the so-called 'warm heart of Africa', reeling off an unbelievable list of excursions he had planned for us in a company car. None of these perks materialised but were great food for thought.

It transpired that we had to go south to Blantyre to pick up the sponsorship money. It also transpired that a Chloride conference, involving MDs from all over Africa, was taking place at Salima over the next few days. Salima is on the edge of Lake Malawi, due east of Lilongwe and about a day's ride.

This conference shed new light on our plans and we set about finding Steve. Somebody in town said they had seen him at the golf club campsite, but on arrival we found no sign of him, his tent or his name in the register. We leapt to the conclusion that Emily, his girlfriend, had just arrived because somebody else said that he had left for the airport that morning; either that or Steve was fed up and going home. We booked ourselves into the campsite, took receipt of our first *cob* and settled down for a quiet day. Very soon we discovered that the entire area was infested with ants, explaining why everybody else was camping one hundred yards further down the slope. Some wet ground under a few trees seemed to be ant-free and the tedium of packing up and repitching our tents took us through to evening. Dave was again persuaded, with difficulty, to ring a 'contact'. The unfortunate victim was Mr B—, an Italian architect who owned a prominent hotel on the southern shores of the lake. According to Dave, this was the man who was going to fly us round the country in his plane and put us up for free in his beautiful hotel. This could not have been further removed from the truth – with great trepidation he had invited Steve to camp in his garden and now found himself extending the invitation to us. We had paid for a night in the campsite, so delayed our invasion for a day, spending the evening doing more research into the merits of Carlsberg as we toasted my brother's wedding which was occurring simultaneously in Hertfordshire.

Mr Bezzarro's house was a red-brick mansion in the centre of town, incorporating grand reception rooms and an enormous swimming pool. The furthest, most secluded corner of his garden became our domain for two days as we collected our spares package and mail. I had asked my mother to send out Proust's *Remembrance of Things Past* and the first thousand pages arrived in one thick volume. I had wanted to read it ever since she had told me that, 'Once you read Proust you'll never look at the world in the same way again'. I started it immediately, unaware of just how big a part of my life it was to become.

The local market was enclosed within a huge oval stadium and sold everything that you would be likely to find in the country – great mounds of fruit and vegetables next to vendors specialising in everything from second-hand bearings to second-hand pieces of metal. The policy of open trading with South Africa was an ironically welcome change from the bleak limitations of Zambia. Supermarkets with food on the shelves were quite an eye-opener. Inevitably our limited funds were squandered on little luxuries like chocolate, especially when out of sight of the equipment manager, who had firmly established himself as finance manager as well. In time it became evident that the equipment manager was more prone to inadvertent indulgences than all of us put together. A forgivable flaw considering the amount of nightmarish jobs he seemed to get lumbered with.

Steve's knee was still on the mend and we watched rather enviously as he drove off to Salima with a Chloride rep. Meanwhile we packed up and tried to leave reasonably early. True to form it was late afternoon before we saddled up, said goodbye to a bewildered B— family and set off. The direct road we had chosen to take was single-track and almost totally devoid of tarmac. As dusk fell we found ourselves slogging up a steep hill listening to an absurd tape just received from a totally crazed friend in London. I felt that we had reached hitherto unrivalled levels of surrealism as the rain came, sweat poured and Hare Krishna chants bellowed from the blaster up front. With headstrong enthusiasm we had elected to take both bikes; an unnecessary piece of masochism since Steve could so easily have taken the mountain bike in the back of a four-wheel drive. Pulling the trailer up long hills, with only two on the trandem, proved particularly intense. The rain gathered momentum as we lost it and soon we were shivering round a fire at the roadside, quaffing ferociously strong home-brewed alcohol with two paralytic locals. However, after an hour the rainclouds had passed, revealing a virtually full moon on the rise. Despite the plethora of potholes, we decided to tackle the road again, covering another forty kilometres. The downhills became longer and steeper as we got closer to the lake and one particularly manic descent left us rather cautiously poised at the top of the next. A car had come hurtling round the corner at the bottom of the hill, headlights on beam, as we came rattling down over potholes and bumps at a good forty miles per hour. We sat down to re-evaluate how sensible we were being, rapidly concluding that we should stay put. An empty irrigation ditch ran off the edge of the road, providing the only flat piece of ground available. We slept with our heads about two feet from the road, praying that drunken bus drivers would choose to crash somewhere else. The moon bathed the bush in crisp metallic light, highlighting the trees with streaks of dulled silver. Undulating hills stretched away towards the lake below, and once again the majestic silence of the African bush shrouded the scene as we drifted off to sleep.

The morning's cycle became a frenzied vortex of anticipation. The closer we came to the lake the harder we hit the pedals. Our first sighting of the bright turquoise water came at the crest of a small hill about half a mile from the shore. Chris and I were on the trandem, fired into overdrive by the habitual screaming Hendrix and virtually frothing at the mouth as we came racing through the gates of the Salima Bay Hotel. Making our way straight through the hotel and across the beach, we ran like demonic swine into the water – the final consummation of months of daydreaming as each mile brought us closer to this lake, which had been elevated to an ethereal paradise in our striving minds. The combination of fine white sand and crystal fresh water was dazzling and disorientating; I had not expected such an idyllic tropical beach.

Steve appeared and immediately informed us that the bar was at our disposal and all orders should be placed on Room 22's bill; our sponsors were really taking care of us. Our space in the campsite became a bombsite; everything from the new spares package and the trailer was spread across the ground. Steve had received a copy of *Avalon Sunset*, Van's latest album, from a friend called Nick in London. Enclosed was a little scrap of paper saying 'Happy cycling – Van Morrison' in swirling blue biro. It transpired that Nick had seen Van in a Notting Hill wine bar and asked him to write a short note to Steve, his friend who was cycling through Africa on the Goodies' trandem. Van obliged and here it was in Steve's hands on a beach in Malawi. He freaked. That scrap of paper was treasured with more care than his passport for the rest of the journey, neatly folded into a compartment of his wallet and produced with great glee upon special request. The new tape was placed in the machine like part of a sacred ritual and I sat down with Steve to listen. It was to prove a turning-point and within days I was an established Vanhead, listening to all the albums Steve had in a new light. Something previously incoherent became lucid and accessible.

The conference spanned four days, at the end of which there would be a big dinner where Three Men on a Bike were to perform a cabaret. This daunting occasion did not receive much attention until just before dinner. Our minstrel was forced to take on his role as 'entertainments manager' by giving a rendition of the theme tune, while we had the embarrassing task of pretending to ride the trandem. Our mime techniques left a lot to be desired and I dread to think how the Chloride executives interpreted our movements as we stood gyrating in a line before them.

The following morning two other cyclists appeared while we were making pathetic attempts to lighten our load and pack the trailer. Christian and Gilly Lee were on their way from Victoria Train Station to Victoria Falls. They had covered many of the roads that we still had to tackle and we started to compare notes. We were rather depressed to learn that they had notched up only one puncture in six thousand miles compared to our thirty-seven in four thousand. As Dave enumerated exactly how many spokes we had broken, wheel rims destroyed and freewheels pulverised, Christian looked down the length of the Goodloid, lying on its back under a jacaranda.

'I'll tell you why you've trashed five freewheels,' he said, 'the frame's twisted.'

Sure enough the rear section of the frame was at a slight angle to the rest, making a straight alignment between the freewheel and the rear chain wheel impossible. The fact that we had failed to notice this ourselves seemed the ultimate proof of our technical ineptitude.

On the first day we had erected our tents without the cover sheets to stay cooler at night. While enjoying access to Room 22's tab, torrential rain burst above us, drenching the tents, sleeping bags and all our clothes. The tents degenerated into sad little wet mounds covered in sand and large rocks to prevent them blowing away. We took to sleeping on a bank tilted towards the beach. A jacaranda tree was silhouetted against the night sky, its huge pods hanging like giant runner beans. One evening we were staring at the changing colours and play of light on the water as the sun sank behind us. Suddenly I noticed a speck of crimson on the horizon. Gradually a pink moon rose from the lake throwing a shimmering silver beam of light across the surface. It felt like the sun had sunk in the west, raced around the globe and reappeared in the east, having lost its power to produce daylight in the process. As it climbed higher the hues mellowed to marigold and finally a pure white moon shone through the drifting clouds, surrounded by rings of sepia like the light at the end of a tunnel. A lashing warm wind blew off turbulent waters, adding to the theatrical extravaganza.

After a couple of relaxing days we started to head south towards Blantyre – a difficult move to make when we still had a few thousand miles to travel north. Steve would have to continue by bus, taking the mountain bike and the equipment we did not need for two days; the swelling on his knee had subsided but it was still too weak for cycling. Christian and Gilly accompanied us to Salima town, where they intended to pick up a bus and we left the trailer in the custody of the police station. As we were about to part ways they reconsidered, and after some gentle persuasion decided to cycle with us. We bought food in the market and in a dusty, golden light headed into the bush. A small clearing beside a waterhole was chosen as our camp for the night and I started cooking a TMOAB pasta special. The moon was rising as we discussed everything from the physical effects of prolonged cycling to the nightmare of returning to London. It was the first time we were able to talk to people in an equatable situation and the vibe between us was good. Christian had been an interior designer and Gilly just so happened to be a documentary editor for the BBC. They sparked off renewed optimism about the film, stressing the importance of various images – elephants in Tanzania, the Masai in Kenya and the pyramids in Egypt. These shots alone could be enough to sell to news programmes on our return. They were a relaxed couple, in their mid-thirties and enjoying their second honeymoon. Their views on everything from neo-colonialism to the advantages of cycling were similar to mine but more lucid and coherent; they had an objective and more mature balance which made me aware of how introspective I had become.

While entrenched in these thoughts and tackling the habitual problem of trying to drain boiling water from pasta without being burnt, I looked up to see about twenty men armed with *pangas* standing around us in a circle. The village headman stood forward.

'Somebody saw you by our waterhole and we came to check that you were not our enemies trying to poison our water.'

We apologised profusely, explained that we were harmless cyclists and showed them the trandem. After looking at the bikes and uttering sighs of disbelief and wonder, they disappeared back into the night with beaming, apologetic smiles.

Dawn shed a pink terracotta light over the bush as we managed to stretch three eggs between the five of us in French toast, greatly enhanced by lemon pepper, a crucial new acquisition. Swapping seats every ten or fifteen miles so Christian and Gilly could try the trandem, we covered long stretches without tarmac. A new surface was being put down and we found ourselves riding through a five-hundred-metre line of workmen; one by one they put down their pickaxes and started dancing and cheering as we drifted through with some reggae playing. I sat at the back slapping hands with them as we passed.

One part of the road came close to the lake on the map and the thought of a midday swim tempted us down a small dirt track to Mulemba. We bought three smoked fish and some vegetables – with some difficulty, since we were surrounded by the entire population of the village, only to learn that it was a cholera area. Denied our swim, we returned to the road and ate under a small shelter infested with ants. The last twelve kilometres to Monkey Bay, the nearest town to Cape Maclear, were very swift; Van was telling us to 'Listen to the Lion' as thin strips of cloud turned crimson and the sun dropped behind a ridge to our left. Monkey Bay held no attraction and we cycled softly out of town, flanked by Christian and Gilly and tuned to the 'Sounds of Silence'. I was feeling euphoric – an overwhelming sense of freedom, comfortably absorbed in the warm, black night and with a vivid impression of my situation. I felt dusty, sweaty and tired; happy, settled and very alive.

For the first time we were struggling to find firewood in the bush. I was entertained by everybody enthusing about peanut butter on Coconut Cookies like it was caviar – I have an intense aversion to peanut butter so I was denied this delicacy. Something large kept rustling in the bush a few feet away as I retreated to sleep. I was surprised to feel no fear.

Cape Maclear is a wide bay with a golden beach and silent water. A set of bungalows and a small restaurant is owned by Mr Stevens and run by a group of sullen young men who have been over-exposed to the steady influx of backpackers and too much commercial profiteering.

A fishing village sprawls along the beach beyond and a small island sits beckoning in the middle of the bay. It was a refreshing change to meet some other travellers but it depressed me as well. I realised just how insular we had become – Christian, Gilly and the other three were the only white people who did not annoy me.

'I'm finding it difficult to relate to anyone except a rural African and you guys,' I had said to Steve a few days earlier. It was a trap of travelling that I had known before. It upset me that I should feel it and I consciously tried to overcome it. If I felt such animosity for western values now, how would I cope with the necessary compromises when we reached London?

A ubiquitous posse of Australians and New Zealanders appeared. Russell looked like the archetypal Aussie, opening beer bottles with his teeth (a technique which Chris adopted), and always wearing a black bushman's hat; however, he was quiet, interesting and perceptive. He was travelling with his girlfriend, Brigitte, and another girl called Kirsty. They had been joined by a twenty-six-year-old New Zealander called Gary Dowling. Gary had grown up on a sheep farm near a place called Taronga on the North Island, had recently been building silos in Sweden and was now making his way up, down and around Africa. He had an endearing smile, an infectious guffawing laugh and the habit of squinting and contorting his face when trying to concentrate. Christian and Gilly meanwhile had taken our advice and headed west to Zambia rather than south through Mozambique.

Somehow a plan was hatched to make a combined trip south from Blantyre to Mount Mulanje and have dinner on the summit – three thousand metres up (about ten thousand feet). Our journey down to Blantyre was unremarkable, except for stopping in Zomba and playing a mad game of golf on a dramatic course surrounded by mountains, and a hairy moment when the brakes failed before a busy roundabout coming into town. Chloride kindly installed us in the Sports Club campsite. On the first evening we bumped into a girl who had been at Edinburgh with Dave and I, which spun me out completely. The next morning we set about straightening the rear forks on the Goodloid. Dave ended up at Brown and Clapperton,

Clockwise from top left:
Dave Elliott,
Rory at work on the first draft on the
banks of the Nile,
Chris Mills,
Steve Corry.

Main picture:
Chris and Dave in the process of successfully destroying another freewheel.

Inset:
Zebra welding the front forks of the Goodloid, prior to the descent into Kariba.

This page, top: Danger! – four wild animals.
Bottom: A moment of respite as Steve fine-tunes the front wheel, just outside Arusha.

Following page, main picture: Roughriding down a donkey track in the Sudan.
Inset: Petrol, Yes?

Stop that train…

Main picture: Time off from Vulcan's forge. Inset: A rare moment of overtaking.

the Malawian cycle manufacturers, with Gary supervising; he was, apparently, a skilled engineer with a 'good knowledge of steel'. The thought of several people heating and bending the Goodloid made me nervous; I was having visions of fractures developing in the frame and the trip being abruptly curtailed. I decided to steer clear and made abortive attempts to sell the Pro Walkman to the Malawian Broadcasting Corporation in a bid to swell our dwindling resources. One sound engineer, with wild mad-professor hair, recommended trying the Ministry of Information. Later that afternoon I found myself sitting at a large desk in a smart office trying to flog my walkman to a member of the Malawian cabinet.

'You see it's very special because you can do high quality recordings; it would be very good for your journalists for example.' I tried my pitch.

'Yes, yes; how do you find Malawi?' he replied.

'Oh, very beautiful and such nice people. Also I can give you this carrying case, the microphone stand and the headphones.'

'Did you like the lake?'

The conversation continued as a hopeless stream of non sequiturs and concluded with an arrangement to meet again after our return from Mulanje.

Gary became so enraptured in the saga of straightening the Goodloid that he suggested cycling up the lake with us on a sponsored bike from Brown and Clapperton. Their bikes are the standard old Raleigh design which are found throughout Africa and known as 'Black Mambas'. Brown and Clapperton were easily convinced by the idea, due to our forthcoming appearance in the national newspapers, and a bike would be available once we had staged the altitude dinner. Gary was christened 'Black Mamba Dowling', which was soon abbreviated to Mamba. He accompanied us to Mulanje, while Russell, Brigitte and Kirsty opted to take the convoy through Mozambique to Zimbabwe, convinced that the altitude dinner was actually a joke.

Mount Mulanje was uncharted territory until Laurens Van der Post wrote about the area in *Venture into the Interior* in the Fifties. We arrived in darkness, unable to see the massif towering above us but feeling its presence. A local porter latched onto us at once; his real name was Wilbur but Dave insisted on calling him Captain Willard – a legacy from his *Apocalypse Now* obsession – and it stuck.

Breakfast was *Howermoot* – South African porridge which claimed to make thirty servings from one small box but provided us only with one meal. Captain Willard was presented with a rucksack full of food while we carried sleeping bags, a new three-man tent which we had acquired through a part-exchange deal in Blantyre, our cooking kit and all the warm clothes we could muster. The trail spiralled gradually up to the lip of the massif, red russet earth bordered by wildflowers and broken by clear, crystal streams. Blisters and cuts on my feet made it impossible to wear boots so I tied the laces together and carried them on my shoulder. It felt good to be barefoot. A deep green gorge dropped down to the right and a bare rock-face caught the sun, streaked with yellow like hills in Provence. Every few minutes we would step to the side and make way for men jogging down the narrow path carrying twenty-foot timber planks on their heads. Despite their exhaustion they invariably greeted us with '*mulumbanji* (good day/hello).'

After an hour the path levelled onto a pine forest plateau; the sun sent stripes of harsh light across the bed of brown needles, which felt like soft carpet underfoot. The air was invigorating, making me want to run everywhere. We stopped for lunch at a log cabin in a clearing called Chembe; a stream of cold water trickled over flat rocks below and you could feel the silence. In the afternoon we continued up through more pine forest before breaking into rugged scrubland reminiscent of the Scottish Highlands. We camped beside the forest on a thick mattress of pine needles; the only water available was provided by a stagnant ditch nearby. Sapwita, the highest peak and our target for the next day, could just be seen in the distance.

I awoke to the sound of Dave's Tarzan calls from the top of an overlooking ridge. The light was hazy and the air was cold. Dense jungle replaced barren moorland as we dropped down into a basin thick with what Van der Post named 'Mulanje Cedars'; although not strictly cedars they do bear some resemblance with their splayed horizontal branches draped with wispy grey-green lichen. The view from the path to the jungle below was like the land that time forgot – the cedars protruded from the canopy of creepers and foliage, the tattered strands of lichen enhancing the primeval atmosphere. A monkey's call, sounding like an amplified Clanger, broke the silence, and I almost expected to see a pterodactyl swooping out of the misty cloud above us. The wildflowers were exotic, deep violets and voluptuous reds. Sinuous moss-covered roots writhed like giant pythons across the path as we now climbed out of the basin. The jungle stopped abruptly and we were back in Scotland. Another two hours on the flat brought us to a corrugated iron shack at the base of Sapwita by about midday.

When we told Captain Willard that we were climbing the peak that afternoon and staying the night up there, his customary grin disappeared for the first time. He looked nervous and insisted that we should go no further until the morning. At first we thought he was worried about the cold and told him that he could sleep in the tent under sleeping bags, which we intended to unzip and use like blankets. He still refused. Eventually we discovered that Sapwita basically means 'don't go there' in the local dialect; he was prepared to go in daylight but nobody was going to make him sleep the night there. We reconsidered and asked him to go back down, buy more food and meet us at the Lachenya hut in the pine forest the following day. His grin returned, more animated than ever, and he charged off downhill, clearly delighted to be rid of us.

Icy water issued from the rocks where we were and we decided to prepare our dinner before the final ascent. Boiling water to cook tagliatelle took forever; meanwhile I soaked the beef in a marinade, adding garlic and chillies. Dave mixed a cocktail of gin and orange squash into water bottles while I strained the tagliatelle and put it in a plastic bag. The next problem was deciding who was carrying what, so we drew lots. Chris, Steve and I took sleeping bags, the tent and clothes, Steve having the extra burden of his guitar tied to his back. Dave looked like a Monty Python waiter, clambering over rocks and through thick scrub, balancing the beef stroganoff and marinade on an outstretched hand, with bottles of water and cocktail in the other. Gary was allotted the unfortunate task of collecting firewood along the way. This motley mountaineering outfit then set off on a three-hour climb to the summit. A sequence of painted red arrows directed us through narrow crevices, up and over huge boulders and into tunnels of scrub on hands and knees. I was still unable to wear boots and found myself jumping gaps between boulders in bare feet and wondering why on earth I had bothered to bring my boots at all. The light was fading when we staggered up to the concrete pillar marking the peak. Bands of orange and mauve covered the sky and a silver sickle moon hung above, flanked by a solitary bright star, reminding me of science fiction films. Steve strummed and sang to the wide open spaces.

TMOAB were all intact but there was no sign of Gary. Half an hour later he tottered out of the bushes, looking like a coalminer, and carrying a vast stack of firewood on his shoulder. His face fell when he looked around to see dry dead branches scattered all over the summit. He had no option but to laugh. Some boulders provided shelter and we lit a fire on a patch on long grass. Dave had managed to drop all the water in a bid to save the stroganoff when he was slipping down a boulder. Consequently the only refreshment was a litre of cocktail which disappeared in under five minutes and left us reeling around the summit in hysterics. Dinner exceeded all expectations. Baked avocados were followed by beef stroganoff with tagliatelle, and fresh pineapple with cream and biscuits. Flaming brandies kept us warm as we pitched the tent on a piece of rock no larger than its base and surrounded by vertical drops. Squeezing five of us into a three-man tent was not easy and I wondered what we would have done about Captain Willard if he had come.

Dawn was spectacular. We sat in crisp cold air watching the mist disperse to reveal the valleys below. The desolate isolation, the pure silence and the panorama of colour created a spiritual tone, making me think about God. With numbed brains we stumbled back down to the base for breakfast. Steve lost all trace of the red arrows and eventually reappeared from further down the mountain, wading through thickets with his guitar, and fuming with frustration after heading for a different stream on a different part of the mountain.

Another four hours took us down to the Lachenya hut near the crest of the massif, crossing streams on small wooden bridges and emerging from lush jungle vegetation into the pine forests. The hut was empty and we made ourselves at home, brewing up tea and lying around smoking. Suddenly an old white battle-axe wandered in from the wilds; immediately we were under fire.

'This is all Mountain Club equipment – you can't use that.'

Nobody really registered what was happening and ignored her rantings; this only incited her more.

'That mug belongs to the Mountain Club,' she bellowed at Chris.

Lethargically, and without saying a word, we evacuated to pitch our tent outside. An hour later I pottered off to a nearby stream with Gary and Dave to have a smoke. She must have thought we were all going to crap in her spring because she accosted us:

'That's our only source and supply of water you know.'

By evening a motley group of hearty walkers had assembled in the hut, having returned from their hearty treks to all corners of the massif – a French doctor, a missionary figure who had been lost in a time warp, his two particularly hearty nieces from England and of course Medusa the ogre, still bustling around and babbling about the Mountain Club. We remained outside, waiting for Captain Willard to return with our food. Steve, bathed in evening sun, sang J.J. Cale songs, and we built a spit for the chicken that Captain Willard delivered just before dusk. He seemed glad that we had survived our night on Sapwita; we paid him for his invaluable help and he shot back down the mountain as darkness closed in.

Choosing a very steep path known as the Boma, the rest of the descent was quick. We paused on flat rocks by idyllic mountain streams before breaking into emerald green tea plantations and finding a bus about to leave for Blantyre. As we drew out from the tea plantations, with the mountain dominating the landscape behind, I immersed myself in visions of returning, but next time with a girlfriend.

We lapsed back into city stagnation for two days in Blantyre. Gary was presented with his Mamba by Brown and Clapperton, complete with solid steel racks and two spare wheels. I enjoyed another fruitless engagement with the Minister for Information before flogging the

Pro Walkman to an Indian for a fraction of its value. We collected our sponsorship from Chloride, attended the press shoot and sent a progress report back to London. A crowded bus took us back to Salima – we arrived at about midnight and strolled into a bar at closing time. A few totally smashed men and women were reeling around, one member of staff was just capable of pushing a broom across the floor while an incessant barrage of noise came blaring from a distorted radio. We spent a warm, comfortable night outside the bus depot with a strong wind blowing. The zip on my sleeping bag had broken in Zimbabwe and I had only just got round to attaching toggle straps down the side so that I could do it up; it was still fairly unpleasant to sleep in however, because the dirt that had accumulated inside was now turning wet and sticky.

After retrieving the trailer from the police station, we set up a bustling bicycle maintenance store at the roadside, replacing the Goodloid's derailleur which had been badly damaged on the roof of the bus, while Gary completed the finishing touches to the Mamba. We set off in mid-morning and were overtaken by an overland truck full of young Australians; we caught them up at the market and freaked them out by explaining that it was the authentic original Goodies' trandem. The Goodies has been re-run several times on Australian television in recent years so they knew what we were on about. We were feeling quite weak, having not cycled for a while, and by mid-afternoon we were looking for possible lakeshore camps. The road over this stretch runs parallel to the lake but a few kilometres inland. Stopping to ask people at the roadside, we discovered that a road by the village of Benga would take us down to the lake, and one man in his twenties volunteered to guide us. A reasonable dirt road soon became a bumpy track and impossible for three of us to ride with the trailer, so I continued solo. The bumpy track soon degenerated into a narrow, muddy path, crossing river beds and dried mud flats which had developed huge cracks in the sun, hardly ideal for our precious rims. We persevered, driven on by the thought of beach and water, until we crossed a shallow ridge into some marshland. Only then did our guide inform us that we had to walk knee-deep through a swamp. It was too late to turn back now but I was reluctant to walk through two hundred yards of swamp with septic, pustulating sores all over my feet. A plague of mosquitos descended and I realised there was little option; Chris and I lifted the trandem above our heads and ploughed into the squelching mud and black, stagnant water. Once we reached the other side, it proved worthwhile. A small Christian fishing village of bamboo and grass huts stretched along a sand peninsula, isolated from the mainland by the swamp and a series of lagoons. A group of elders stood in a circle singing hallelujahs and white light bounced off the surf. Our guide was the only English speaker around and also the owner of the only small shop, conveniently situated a few paces from a little empty hut which we were shown to. It was not long before we had exhausted his supply of biscuits. A peaceful evening developed and I became further entranced by Van the Man. I think you almost 'learn to like' Van – his music is on such a pure and idiosyncratic level that you need to identify with him before something rambling and incoherent becomes emotive and soulful. Beyond the actual lyrical content there is something innately ethereal about his music, that indefinable quality which constitutes a real artist.

I filmed the trek back across the swamp – little children carrying our panniers above their heads and pockets of mist hovering on the water. The ride to Nkhota Kota – supposedly the largest traditional town in Central and Southern Africa – drifted by effortlessly for TMOAB. Not so for Gary, slogging away on the heavily laden Mamba, and we started to rotate all five positions every fifteen miles. We camped under a big tree on the beach and were joined by an old fisherman called Banda, who showed us how to cook fried fish to perfection. *Chambo* and *kampanga* were the only edible fish we came across in Malawi; the former resembled bream and the latter a large catfish. Strong moonlight shone through the tree as we ate and shadows from the leaves created dancing patterns on the white sand.

We applied the name of the Slow-But-Sure-Grocery in the market to our progress through Malawi and continued to meander up the edge of the lake; a better road ran further inland but we were too accustomed to the luxury of camping on beaches with an inexhaustible supply of freshwater to even think about an alternative route.

The road surface deteriorated as we cycled north and quite often we were forced to dismount and walk through a few kilometres of soft sand. The landscape started to undulate, occasionally revealing green hills draped in mist to the west, bushfires and dramatic sunsets adding an apocalyptic feel.

A moon-cycle, through a stretch of what was supposedly a game park, was particularly memorable. We were joined by an old man on a South African bike called a 'Bomber' – he'd broken and lost his chain on a bridge so we lent him our spare until we reached his house at the end of the game park. Once again we saw no evidence of any game whatsoever, except a pack of wild dogs which chased Dave on the mountain bike. The ride reminded me of cycling out of Monkey Bay with Christian and Gilly – the complete tranquillity, no people in the villages and no sounds in the bush, just the gentle purr of the tyres on tarmac as we floated through a silver landscape, stealthily, like animals. At midnight we pulled over under a tree in the middle of a village.

Conveniently we woke to find ourselves opposite a restaurant; we had breakfast and covered ten kilometres into Dwangwa. Somebody had told us about this village when we were in Kariba, claiming that all the children there had been killed by malaria. We had assumed he was exaggerating but unfortunately he was not; it was stark, deathly and devoid of children. It also marked the end of all tarmac until Nkhata Bay, two hundred kilometres further north, and we launched straight into corrugations and sand. After an hour's walk we stopped for a drink at a small gathering of huts; apparently, a few kilometres further on, there was a beautiful beach called Ngara, where there were 'cottages for strangers'. This immediately destroyed any aspirations of a hard day's cycle.

The Ngara 'cottages for strangers' were run by a man called Charles who insisted on calling us all 'master' and asking whether we wanted 'African tobacco'. A whitewashed cottage with thatched roof, a verandah and five beds became our home for two days and cost two pounds between five of us. Dazzling pink bougainvillea covered a long-drop loo outside and parched grass stretched down to shady trees and the beach.

On the first morning Dave concocted scrambled eggs, complete with a liberal sprinkling of 'African tobacco'. An hour later I was pinned to the beach, moaning like a delirious invalid, while gravity seemed to exert double its normal force on my lifeless limbs. In this dilapidated state I took up the challenge of the TMOAB board game and the day developed into a distant blur. Charles produced some home-brewed alcohol which gave me a ferocious stomach ache and did little to alleviate the mayhem.

A stunning light had developed by evening, turning turquoise water to opalescent mercury as the water gradually calmed to a rhythm of regulated ripples, ebbing softly against the shore. At the time I could not envisage a more perfect place to live – fresh lakeshore breezes blowing from open horizons, beautiful white sand beaches, uncorrupted people and a never-ending supply of delicious fish and disease-free drinking water. It sounds pretty good now actually.

Ngara was a hard place to leave after two days; we succeeded by making an early start and leaving no time for anyone to say: 'Maybe we should stay another day'. The road was the worst we had encountered; deep sand leading onto a hard surface made with half-embedded stones and covered with huge scattered rocks. It was not long before we had destroyed a wheel on the back of the Goodloid. We changed wheels in the next village and covered another few miles, mostly walking, before stopping to camp in a village.

I woke to find that I had slept with my head on a scorpion all night. We breakfasted on the new TMOAB special; unable to suss out a way to wash and strain rice with our limited kitchen, we had stopped trying and resorted to adding sugar, bananas and ginger. The entire village assembled to watch us leave and I filmed Dave skanking with an old woman. Midday temperatures were the hottest we had known and we were plagued with breakdowns. The Wonderful Wheel of Ninon kept tightening on itself, causing us either to grind to a halt or struggle on laboriously, putting maximum strain on all the parts. Chris took to walking the trailer like a dog on a lead while the rest of us dismantled the hub. We ended up walking the rest of the way to the Chintchechwe Inn where we found another even more beautiful beach.

Since Steve was so accustomed to tuning guitars, he had always been given the task of tuning the rear wheel on the Goodloid, a job that frequently happened several times a day. His capacities as a wheel specialist were now stretched to the limit as he sat down to construct a wheel from scratch for the first time. Reclining on the beach with a pile of spokes, a hub and an empty wheel rim, using a tiny illustration from a tattered segment of the *Readers Digest Cycle Maintenance Manual*, he managed to build a wheel which went on to cover hundreds of miles.

Unable to remove the freewheel from the old wheel, we walked a few kilometres to a garage and used their vice. Steve and I were pulling the trailer over sand and gravel as patches of morning sun were diffused through the trees.

'How do you feel about God these days?' I suddenly asked.

'Well, it's funny you should say that – I've been thinking about him quite a lot actually.'

'Yeah? That's weird – so have I – especially since Mulanje.'

We had both travelled in India before and we started to draw comparisons. The spiritual atmosphere in India is so pervasive, so up-front for all to see, that you can never escape it. Every scene encapsulates an innate mystical awareness. However, trying to understand, let alone assimilate, the complexities of Hinduism, requires a conscious effort to embrace a culture. In Africa one is confronted with Nature. It is a subtle, passive spirituality that seeps around you in the bush, embodied in silence, or hits you more directly in the form of long horizons, some barren and desolate, others fertile and inhabited but harmoniously merged with nature; food, building materials and farming tools are all drawn directly from the earth. No religion has spread comprehensively through sub-Saharan Africa; Christianity and Islam have thrived in some areas but the population density is so small and the distances so great that nothing has ever managed to permeate every level and replace the traditional, localised belief systems of primal religions; animism and ancestor worship were very much alive in the villages where we stayed.

The road to Nkhata Bay took us over rolling, misty hills; it corresponded more to how I had imagined Malawi. We paused by a small clearing on the crest of a hill, where the grave of a village chief lay in peaceful sanctuary; clouds of smoke drifted serenely across the tree tops in the valley behind. The road continued through terraced rubber plantations, where we stopped to talk with an old man called Chester from the hills. The first stretch of tarmac since Dwangwa signalled our arrival in Nkhata Bay and we coasted down a winding road which overlooked the blue water below.

A promontory separates the small town of Nkhata Bay from the beach. Similar to Cape MacLazy, it attracts a relentless stream of backpackers and overlanders, the majority of whom stay at the Heart Motel in town and walk over the ridge to the beach. The last contingent of resident sunbathers were on their way back as we pushed the bikes over ruts and rocks to find an empty beach. Reports were rife about theft, so we used the bikes as a stockade around some rocks which protruded into the water and were overhung by two small trees. The moon rose about nine, climbing up behind the rocks, silhouetting the trees against the night sky and casting a constant beam of light across calm water.

We stayed for a few days, savouring our last opportunity to relax by the lake before tackling the long distances in Tanzania. The water was flat and calm throughout, especially so at dawn when it looked like a huge sheet of glass covering an aquarium. Fishermen drifted past in their dugouts, occasionally stopping to sell us something for dinner that night. It became my favourite time to swim, cutting a path through a placid surface to rocks at each end of the cove.

Various groups of travellers gradually appeared and were given quite a shock on our first morning. Fort Goodloid already covered a fair part of the beach and was being extended to include the area around a shelter, which the equipment manager had started whipping up after breakfast. A group of young children had volunteered to do our washing for a few *kwatcha* and our wet clothes were now strewn across the sand, making almost half the beach impassable. Steve was playing guitar on the rocks, Hare Krishna chants were bellowing from the blaster, Dave was hacking down undergrowth for the roof of his shelter, Chris was whirling ebony nunchukkas around his head, Gary was trying to write a letter and I was reading Proust; it must have looked like a Dadaist play.

On the fourth day an English couple appeared in a Land Rover and set up camp at the other end of the beach. They were both vets and were coming to the end of a six-month trip which had taken them across the Sahara and into the heart of Zaire; they planned to relax on the beach for a few days before selling the vehicle in Lilongwe and flying home. We warned them about the local thief, who was still at large but had spared us so far. A small party developed at our end of the beach and several people slept around Fort Goodloid. About four in the morning I awoke to find people jumping over the top of me and tearing down the beach clutching assorted weapons; cries for help were coming from the Land Rover. The psychotic thief had slashed into their tent with a *panga*. Trying to defend his wife, the man had raised his hand and received a powerful blow from the knife, which had shattered his knuckles and left a deep wound. He leapt out of the tent to find the lunatic coming back at him. The sound of ten people stampeding down the beach deterred the attacker and he disappeared without trace into the jungle behind. Daylight revealed the extent of the attack – their tent was in tatters and I was surprised that they had survived.

In the middle of this nocturnal excitement, Steve had been stumbling around in a delirious state – he had malaria. These recent developments indicated a move from the beach to the Heart Motel. Steve was installed into Room 1A, a dark, dank and depressing little hole covered in corrugated iron, where he could watch the flies buzz around his sweating brow. Meanwhile we prepared for the road ahead, stripping both bikes down outside the hotel. Assuming that Steve would need at least a week to recover, we planned to continue with Gary in his place, having sold the Mamba in nearby Mzuzu. We walked up the long hill out of town at dusk; fireflies lined the roadside like flashing lights on a dancefloor. At the top of the hill was a large tree and a small shop owned by an old man called Running. I was feeling tired and irritable; the cuts on my feet were still festering and matters were made worse when I stepped in dogshit twice in five minutes. I sought refuge in my sleeping beauty, sinking into an introverted, self-alienated mood.

The day started with a long downhill and a puncture. It continued with a sequence of long uphills and the demise of a trailer tyre. I started feeling weak and worthless, falling asleep at the roadside and being feverish. I decided to hitch ahead to Mzuzu and have a malaria test. A Belgian couple in a Land Cruiser picked me up and dropped me near to the hospital. They were unable to give me a test until later so I tottered into town and entrusted the mountain bike to a particularly fascist-looking officer at the police station. Convinced that I now had malaria as well, I waited in the centre of town until the others arrived. We decided that I should get a bus back to Nkhata Bay, recover with Steve, and then meet up again in Iringa, four hundred kilometres into Tanzania. While they set about repairing the trailer tyre, I staggered up to the bus stop and found that no buses were going until that evening. I stumbled back across town, collapsed beside the road and tried to hitch. A few hours later the sun was setting and I had not moved. I felt vulnerable, alone and very ill. Feeling faint, I ambled back to the bus stop and was spotted by Dave; the tyre had been stitched together by a man at the roadside mending shoes, and they were about to head out of town. They helped me fight my way onto a crowded bus, where I buried my head into my folded arms, tumbling out at Nkhata Bay late that night and finding my way back to Room 1A and my malarial companion.

The Heart started to empty out the following morning and we moved from the misery of Room 1A to the relative bliss of 'malaria cottage', a small whitewashed hut with two beds. We did nothing for nine days except sweat, listen to music, sweat, moan and groan about the World-interesting-Service, sweat more and play battleships. Steve hit the road to recovery with a course of chloroquine. I tried the same, felt better and then deteriorated to worse than before. My face turned a pale shade of grey and deep craters developed around my eyes. I resorted to a course of Fansidar, a stronger drug which does irreparable damage to your liver but seemed to do the trick. After three days we ventured a few hundred yards into town, broke into feverish sweats and realised that we were still far from full strength. We started our rehabilitation programme, which gave us license to eat as many pancakes as possible smothered in condensed milk and jam.

Our only companions at the Heart were a Kiwi called Tony and the hotel staff. Tony had taken a canoe down the Congo and was now trying to buy a dugout to take down the lake. The staff kept us amused, especially a Hendrix lookalike with round shades, a headband and a repertoire of wonderful English expressions. Coffee fell into short supply on the second day and whenever I asked for some, he would say: 'Sorry for coffee'. Several little skankers ran around trying to make a few *tambala* by getting us cold drinks; otherwise it was quiet and empty, reminiscent of staying on at school after the end of term.

Mamba Dowling reappeared. He had cycled as far as Karonga, near the Tanzanian border, where Chris and Dave had left the trailer for us to pick up. Chris had been very weak and ill for a day in Livingstonia, but seemed to recover quickly. They still planned to meet us in Iringa. Mamba stayed a night and then headed south. His plans changed incessantly and it had become an in-joke; every day he would sit staring at our map and every day he had a new plan.

'I think I might head west actually – git me guitar sent down to Zim, meet me mate Spider and then head north to Nairobi.'

The following day it would be different.

'I think I might cycle to Nairobi with you boys, pick up me guitar and head west to Zaire.'

Steve, Tony and I cooked chickens on the beach on our last night. The water was choppier than before and the light less vibrant – the changing patterns of nature. At five the next morning we caught the bus to Mzuzu, changed twenty dollars, picked up the mountain bike and walked to the northern edge of town to try and score a lift. Unbelievably, the first vehicle to stop was going to Iringa – an old cattle truck with a trailer behind, filled with forty-four-gallon drums, old towing cable and polythene covered in tar which I repeatedly stepped in. We made ourselves comfortable on an oil drum and settled into feeling like Kerouac beatniks from *On the Road*. The road was mountainous, giving us spectacular views of the lake which turned from cobalt blue to slate grey as dusk descended. I tried to retrieve the trailer from the police in Karonga but was told to come back in the morning. We ate in a truckers' café with our driver and his mate, who were both Tanzanian, before clearing a space to sleep in the back of the truck. My feet were covered in sticky black tar, I was tired and dirty and the bottom of my sleeping bag was soaked in diesel. It felt great to be travelling again.

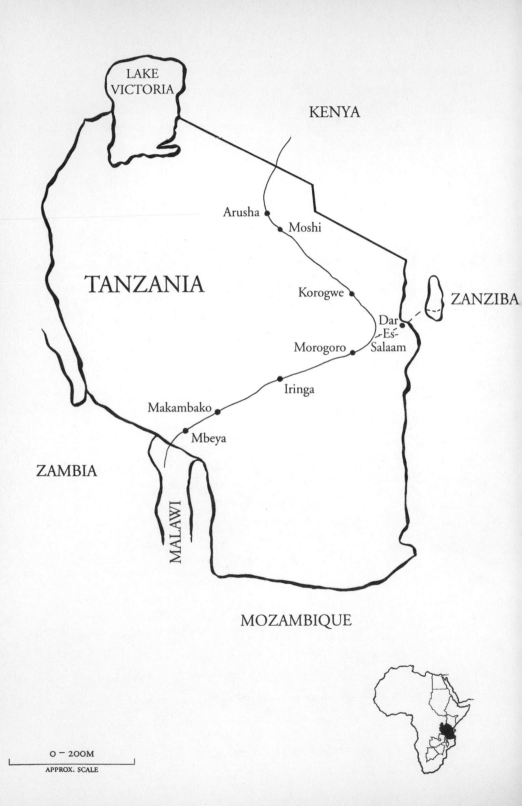

LAKE
VICTORIA

KENYA

TANZANIA

Arusha

Moshi

Korogwe

Dar
Es
Salaam

ZANZIBA

Morogoro

Iringa

Makambako

Mbeya

ZAMBIA

MALAWI

MOZAMBIQUE

O — 200M
APPROX. SCALE

Tanzania

Our image of Tanzania had been tainted by so many reports of stealing that it had already become referred to as 'Tanzathief'. The only people who seemed to have enjoyed it were Christian and Gilly. This is easily explained – most of the people we talked to had come from the security of saturated tourism in Kenya, stopped in Dar-es-Salaam and, having been ripped off on the black market, decided they hated Tanzania and took a bus or train straight into the comfort of 'Mellowi'. What they had missed was everything that Christian and Gilly had been exposed to by cycling – the heaven and hell of a beautiful country in decay.

The officials at the border set a precedent for what was to follow. First of all a dictatorial health officer noticed that our cholera vaccinations had just expired – we must return to Karonga, have a vaccination (which is now considered useless anyway), and then come back. Alternatively the situation could be resolved by paying him a 'small favour'.

'Fat chance you bad skanker,' muttered Steve.

After five minutes he realised that nobody was getting any 'small favours' out of us and relented. We proceeded to Immigration.

'Ah yes, you must each change fifty US dollars.'

We were expecting this.

'Ah no, you see we are part of a sponsored expedition for charity.'

Producing various press cuttings as proof, we managed to escape by agreeing to change fifty dollars between us when we reached a bank. The customs officer was predictably fat and belligerent but was unable to find our concealed currency.

Our truck wound slowly up a steep gravel road which levelled to reveal some of the most breathtaking scenery of the trip. Everything suddenly seemed on a bigger scale than ever before and I felt that we had just entered the real Africa – rounded spurs intersecting with sinuous valleys which stretched to distant horizons; fertile terraced plots of vivid greens and rich browns, producing tea and the biggest bananas that I have ever seen. The dirt road turned to tarseal, splattered with cavernous potholes. The cultivated terraces continued with ripening golden maize as we passed through small villages. A slipping clutch had been causing problems and now called it a day, bringing us to a halt on a shallow incline. The driver and his sidekick crawled underneath, gave the gearbox a cursory glance, rolled a joint and sat back to wait for help. Their English was limited but we managed to deduce that the wait could be a matter of days and not hours.

A regular sight over recent months had been immobilised trucks beside the road, skirted by a few branches pulled from the bush and acting as hazard signs, half an engine or gearbox lying in pieces on the ground and the drivers asleep in the shade. Only now did I realise that these guys would be waiting for up to several days for someone to reappear with spares. As we started unloading the mountain bike and trailer, an overland truck appeared; with obvious signs of reluctance it pulled over. While trying to cram everything onto an already overladen vehicle, the Iringa-bound bus came grinding uphill and joined the party. A frantic scene developed as I tried to hold back an impatient bus driver and load the bike and trailer onto the roof, only to remember that we had no Tanzanian shillings. While Steve hassled the overlanders for cash and got seriously burnt on the exchange rate, I tried to prevent a fuming bus driver and disgruntled crowd of passengers from tearing off into the distance with all our possessions. This frenzy was resolved and we settled in for a fourteen-hour trip to Iringa with no money, no food and no water. At one stop the sight of food was too much for us to bear and we swopped a shirt for four samosas. The first town was Tukuyu and we were deliberating whether to shed more clothes for more samosas when I caught sight of Chris and Dave wheeling the trandem into the Three In One Guest House. Another frantic episode ensued as we unloaded our equipment and tried to get a refund for our tickets from a despairing driver.

Chris and Dave had been attacked and robbed the night before; Tanzathief was living up to its reputation. They had camped in one of the linear villages which had seemed so peaceful and prosperous in this fertile landscape. In the middle of the night they woke to find a man peering into the tent brandishing a big knife and announcing, 'I am police-ing you'. Dazed, confused and trapped by the confines of their sleeping bags, they had little option but to watch him pass the panniers out to his accomplices, who then disappeared in the darkness. Dave had his nunchukkas at the back of the tent and started feeling around for them. Thinking that there was money concealed there, the thief ordered them out of the tent. His ranting pretence about being a policeman had been replaced by a plain and simple 'I kill you'. Dave found his chukkas and sprang out of the tent, receiving a cut between his thumb and forefinger. Scared by this retaliation, the thief ran off through the trees, hotly pursued by Chris wielding the cooking grill above his head and screaming abuse into the night.

Steve and I were taken through the ordeal in graphic detail, characteristically embellished by Dave, which sparked visions of similar incidents happening every night. The two panniers they had taken contained all our specialised tools and spares, most of which were totally useless to anyone else in Africa and without which we were effectively immobile. The other major loss was the Nikon camera. In the morning we were having breakfast in the market when a woman approached Chris and told him that she had overheard the thieves talking about the robbery on a bus that morning. The local police were already on the case and this new information led to them arresting several suspects and arranging an identity parade. Each man was told to say 'I am police-ing you' to Chris and Dave who had great difficulty in suppressing their laughter in a room full of authentic policemen. Nothing developed from this farcical scenario and we resigned ourselves to continuing without tools, spares or our camera.

From Tukuyu we dropped down into a valley at high speed. A blow-out near the bottom sent us snaking across the road at forty miles per hour, resorting to the soles of our boots to bring us to a halt on a bridge. While we were patching up a massive hole in the inner tube, a man on a motorbike drew up beside us.

'It is our policy in Tanzania not to trust foreigners,' he said dogmatically. 'You must move away from the bridge otherwise people will think that you are here to blow it up.'

In the light of recent events it was hardly our policy to trust Tanzanians, but we complied. The road started to climb again and we succumbed to long stretches of walking. The malaria had sapped my strength and I felt weak, breathless and irritable. We cooked lunch under a bamboo shelter and the kindness of a mellow old man reaffirmed our faith in the good nature of the rural African. We passed through one small town bustling with a vibrant clothes market where the rich, warm colours reminded me of India. Long steep inclines took us out of fertile valleys and into dry alpine scenery; white chalk replaced rich red earth and lush long grass turned to soft cushions of short moss. The tarmac had disappeared and we walked on cement-grey gravel to the peak of an escarpment, where we were rewarded with a view down to the plains ahead, the town of Mbeya and another range of bluish hills behind. A weird spacey atmosphere pervaded in the harsh high altitude light; it felt empty and still.

I was pleased to be having my stint on the mountain bike – I was feeling depressed and wanted solace. The road swept downhill for a few miles and I enjoyed an effortless and fast freewheel, feeling the wind howl around me as I looked at the vast panorama below. I finally came to rest by a stream at the bottom, expecting to see the trandem hurtling round corners and weaving past potholes. After five minutes there was no sign of it and, fearing the worst, I started an arduous slog back up the hill. A pick-up truck then appeared with three beaming faces and the trandem in the back. The rear tyre had exploded at forty-five miles per hour and sent them slewing across the road into potholes; the wheel was totally trashed and it took two hundred yards with all feet on the ground to bring them to a stop. They escaped unscathed which, considering the vertical drops at the roadside, was a near miracle.

Mbeya is a big, sprawling town converging on the most prominent hill in the range which forms this part of the Great Rift Valley. We had met a well-educated and erudite young Tanzanian called Charles while in Tukuyu. He ran an export business based in Mbeya and insisted on taking us for dinner at the Rift Valley Hotel. Over the next two days we sent telexes to London to try and get new spares, tools and a camera sent out to Dar-es-Salaam; we combed the market for any sign of the stolen goods, scraped together a temporary tool kit and received endless hospitality from Charles. Malaria, now affectionately referred to as 'Malcolm', was still making its presence felt in my brain and bloodstream. When we left Mbeya on Friday the 13th of October, I was feeling almost normal. We battled our way into a headwind which would be a hindrance over the next eight hundred kilometres to Dar. The land became increasingly arid – burnt charcoal bushland and desolate black villages with no water; the fertile valleys of the Tukuyu region felt a million miles away and Lake Malawi seemed like more of a paradise than ever. It was the poorest and most depressing region we had seen and the people had none of the vitality and animation which we had been so accustomed to. An air of security, prosperity and life had been replaced by one of danger, poverty and death. We stopped in Chimala and felt a hostility which until now had seemed impossible. An old man with an extraordinary, almost albino, complexion took us in and dispersed the crowds of antagonising children; he was a peaceful but solemn character, sustained by nostalgia and living in his past. He staggered around, spluttering from excessive smoking, and his nostrils seemed to have merged into one from years of snuff abuse. He seemed alienated from the community and I felt sorry for him.

A misty morning gave way to another howling headwind. Stopping in the shade at Igawa for some lunch, we found two men wandering round the market, whipping people with bamboo canes. When we asked why these unfortunate people were being subjected to this, we were just told that they were 'being useless' – very weird. As we ate stale chapatis under a tree, we got talking to a Somali truck

driver. He told us about thieves near Iringa, who jump on the back
of lorries grinding slowly uphill, and throw everything off the back.
I developed surreal visions of people leaping onto our trailer and
stealing Steve's guitar.

Loose cranks were becoming more and more of a problem without
our tools and much time was wasted looking for 14 mm spanners
in little villages. We found a Finnish geologist from Dar University
sitting on his Land Cruiser at the top of a hill and smoking a pipe.
He gave us cold water and extended an invitation to dinner when we
reached Dar.

Midday temperatures were higher every day and sweat was leaving
salt stains encrusted across T-shirts and headbands. This stretch was
rapidly asserting itself as the most strenuous to date. Understandably,
Chris and Dave had been reluctant to camp in the bush since the
robbery. All small towns had cheap guest-houses but now we found
ourselves adrift in the bush as the light faded. We decided to walk
to a nearby village and ensure our safety by presenting ourselves to
the local CCM. President Nyerere had introduced the CCM system
throughout the country – basically a district council to assist local
government. Going through a frustrating process of explaining who
we were to an assembled group of elders, we managed to break
through what seems to be an innate xenophobia. Our spiel about
African Medical Research seemed to impress them but thereafter they
remained convinced that we were doctors.

In the morning, taking what we thought was a short cut back to
the road, we walked six miles through thorny scrub before finding
tarmac again. The headwind was now so intense that it was a struggle
to go faster than walking speed. We walked into Makambako after
thirty unbearably frustrating, miserable and silent miles. Cranks were
coming loose so regularly that full surgery was required. We found a
corner in the market and, under siege from an enormous crowd, took
everything apart, borrowing tools from a truck driver doing repairs
nearby. By three in the afternoon we were ready to move. Within a
mile the crank was loose again. We tightened the locking ring with
a nail and continued. Two hundred yards later we noticed a wobble
developing in the rear wheel. Two spokes were broken, one of them

on the freewheel side. Lightheartedly we set about removing the freewheel using the multigrips and brute force. Within five minutes we had succeeded in breaking it. A crisis situation was brewing up fast and we checked into the Lutheran Guest House on the edge of town.

At a workshop the next morning we discovered that everything that could be out of alignment was out of alignment and that the weary Goodloid was bent in the middle. Other revelations included a chain on the verge of collapse and bent chain rings on the rear crank, which had somehow relocated itself at an angle to the frame. Things were looking decidedly bad. We were unable to proceed and walking seven hundred kilometres to Dar pushing a broken Goodloid was a ludicrous option. Dave and I tried to telephone Dar but found that we needed a hundred and twenty-one shilling coins to make a three-minute call. To complicate matters further we found that the trains to Dar were fully booked except for a slim chance of three seats in second class that evening. A spoof was called to send one person ahead to Dar. Predictably Dave was packing his bags five minutes later and within half an hour he had secured a lift. Meanwhile Chris was looking and feeling very ill. Steve and I went to the station to try and secure tickets; the train was not due for another eight hours but chaos was already brewing and we decided to try and hitch. After three hours of sitting beside the road Chris had gone totally grey and started throwing up blood. The situation was becoming absurd and we retreated to the Lutheran Guest House where we found a Swedish nurse on her way to a mission hospital in the bush. She checked Chris out and diagnosed malaria combined with acute dehydration; if we put him on a train for fifteen hours he might die. He needed to be treated immediately and the only option was the mission hospital. Clutching all our clean needles, Chris was bundled into a Land Rover and taken away; everything happened so quickly that we hardly had time to question what was going on. Steve and I adjourned to a bar and tried to quell our paranoia about letting Chris go on his own – we had developed horrific images of this hospital in the bush.

Resigned to travelling third-class, we manoeuvred both bikes and the trailer onto the platform. The station swarmed with heavily armed soldiers and army trucks, making us feel like escaped POWs. The train clattered in on time and I loaded the bikes into the guards' van, using every chain and padlock we had to make them secure. The guard then tried to insist that the Goodloid was three bicycles and charge me accordingly; this threw me into a tantrum and after a torrent of abuse he relented.

We woke to a wild sunrise in the middle of the Selous Game Reserve; groups of wildebeest, gazelles, zebra and giraffe were catching the morning sun as we passed through stretches of open bushland. One giraffe turned and bolted away from the train, its coat shimmering in the light. I never realised that a giraffe in motion could be so fluid and graceful.

Les Evans had contacted the Rotary Club in Dar on our behalf and Dave had already been in touch with one of their leading members, John Oyer. We were picked up from the station and driven straight to his house for lunch. He proved to be a relaxed, jovial businessman with a harem of wives to cook for him and a stomach to show for it. I have never seen so much food placed in front of four people – mountains of rice, beef dishes, chicken dishes, salads and ratatouille – all washed down with a bottle of three-star brandy. We ate and drank accordingly, suffering severe indigestion all afternoon. In this bloated state we were driven to our new home, the garden of a prominent rotarian called J.J., whose palatial house is situated on Mikocheni beach about seven miles from the centre of town. J.J.'s garden actually became the most depressing camping location to date; it extended across a swamp which separated our abode from his house, and which must be one of the most prolific mosquito breeding grounds in East Africa. Contrary to what one might expect, daylight provided no respite and the little nightmares attacked incessantly twenty-four hours a day. After seeking sanctuary on the beach one would return to find them festering and breeding in the shower, eager to dive-bomb the first piece of white flesh they could find. Matters were made more miserable by the arrival of the rains, rendering all available firewood unusable and making it impossible for us even to brew tea, let alone cook anything. The cycle of misfortune, which had been gathering momentum since Nkhata Bay, was showing little sign of relenting.

Life lapsed into intermittent trips to town to try and 'get things together'. Dar reminded me of Indian cities – the ocean boulevards of Bombay, the markets of Calcutta and the winding streets of Old Delhi. Indian and Islamic influences were evident in crumbling façades and the rambling streets were lined with dusty, dirty sand like melting slushy snow. Street stalls and hawkers were everywhere, offering everything from 'brown sugar' to black market exchange rates. As Steve and I discovered, changing money in Dar-es-Salaam was something to be approached with extreme caution. After some initial attempts with blatantly crooked hustlers in the town centre, we ventured further afield to a street stall where Steve had been offered a sensible rate.

Convinced that we were 'nobody's fool when it comes to changing money' we strolled boisterously into the lion's den. We found ourselves in the back seat of a taxi, parked in a prominent position on the corner of Samora Avenue, the main street in Dar; it stank of deceit and danger from the word go. Bundles of small notes were passed back for us to count and a huge pile of cash started to collect around our feet. When we had about twenty thousand Tanzanian shillings littered around the floor, a man appeared on the pavement and poked his head through the window.

'I am a policeman – what are you doing?' he asked Steve.

'Well, I was trying to get a taxi and this man just started handing me all this money,' was his nervous explanation.

I realised quite quickly that this man was about as likely to be a policeman as he was to be my grandmother; for a start his accomplice was wearing a T-shirt emblazoned with a logo saying 'Ganja University'. Fortunately my first move had been to unlock the door on my side and I started to edge my way out onto the street, only to be accosted by a group of seven thugs who now surrounded the car and were threatening to take Steve off to the 'police station'. Aware that Steve was as good as dead in a gutter if they drove off, I started to push people away from the car, pulling the Ganja University student's arm up into a half-nelson and allowing Steve room to escape. We sprinted off down the street and the sterling concealed in my shoe fell onto the pavement – fortunately I noticed, and ran back to retrieve it, finding time to hurl abuse back towards the taxi. With huge rushes of adrenalin we marched back to meet the others, before suffering intense paranoia as I tried changing money again with someone who actually proved reliable and genuine.

An emaciated and anaemic Chris reappeared from the wild. With typical nonchalance he told us how he had narrowly escaped death from an air bubble in a saline drip and that the hospital had no clean needles. He seemed in high spirits but soon fell victim to the 'J.J. garden depression syndrome'. We presumed, prematurely, that fate was smiling on us again when we secured a sponsorship deal with BP. They produced sixty thousand of the hundred thousand shillings we had requested – about three hundred pounds and enough to contemplate a few days in Zanzibar while waiting for our new tools, spares and camera to arrive. However, the next two days confirmed that this black period was far from over. Firstly I received a telex through the High Commission saying that all the film I had shot since Zimbabwe was unusable due to the camera developing the same problem as before. The one concrete thing I had hoped to achieve this year had suddenly vaporised; I felt there was no point in trying to continue and resigned myself to selling the equipment. The following day my depression was replaced by a hollow emptiness. I called my mother to ask for a cooker to be included in the spares package, only to discover that a friend had died of an asthma attack while in Kashmir with her boyfriend, who is also a close friend. I spent the afternoon staring into the Indian Ocean and all I could see was her face.

The next day malaria struck again. I had no option but to lie in the shade by the mosquito swamp and continue to get bitten. I gulped down a course of Fansidar and regained my strength on the second day, having concluded that life was depressing. In an attempt to blow the blues away, we decided to take a dhow to Zanzibar. The boats leave at the convenient hour of three a.m. so we headed into town to see if we could stay at the AMREF headquarters for the few hours before departure. We waltzed in and announced ourselves as Three Men on a Bike but were dismayed to find that nobody there had ever heard of us despite the fact that we had raised several thousand pounds for them. In the next few hours I developed amoebic dysentery; this was going beyond a joke. Suffering from severe stomach cramps and with little control of my bowels, I stuffed my shorts with loo paper and boarded the dhow for what promised to be the most intense journey I could imagine. The boat was so full that it proved impossible to lie down, let alone find a loo. I secured a position at the side, clenched my buttocks together and sat tight for ten hours.

Dolphins leapt from the wake as dawn broke. We sneaked past customs and immigration and set about finding a beach where we could camp. Apparently camping was illegal, so we made our way to the most obscure part of the island we could find. Even then we were collared by a Zanzibar Tourist Official, who refused us permission to camp but showed us to a house we could rent as long as we paid in hard currency. After a long haggle we made a deal, paying him local currency in return for his ignoring our presence. The beach was not spectacular and the nearest village was a desolate place full of deformed mongrels. The redeeming feature was the abundance of unbelievably cheap seafood – we bought the largest lobster I have ever seen for under two pounds.

One morning I bought a three-foot octopus and was sitting on the verandah of our house cleaning it.

'God, I wish I knew how to make sushi,' I said to Steve.

Half an hour later a couple appeared on the beach, a Japanese girl with a Tanzanian boyfriend. Hearing Steve's guitar and singing, they wandered over and we started talking.

'Do you know how to make sushi?' I asked her, half-joking.

'Yeah, sure.'

In total shock I watched her remove the thin rubbery skin and meticulously clean a tentacle. Then she pulled a plastic lunch box from her bag and produced genuine Japanese soy sauce and two parcels of rice wrapped in seaweed. Five minutes later I had a piece of sushi in my mouth. It transpired that her husband, who was currently in Japan, was setting up a business in Zanzibar cultivating seaweed and that she had crucial ingredients for Japanese food sent over; bizarre.

Our return from Zanzibar was more comfortable for all of us except Steve who had notched up his next dose of malaria. He went ghostly pale and spent most of the trip poised over the back of the boat being sick as the engine coughed diesel fumes into his face. Life at the mosquito swamp continued in the customary vein. We were kept amused by Mr Bakari, the gatekeeper and gardener, who shuffled around with a constant smile repeating the only English he knew: 'J.J. – the house – the house – J.J.'. Another distraction was The Family Resort – a misleading name for a bar that was effectively a brothel and where we found some new friends. In these times of trouble, trying to overcome temptation while surrounded by beautiful young black girls was not easy.

The arrival of the spares felt like Christmas. In addition to a new camera, tools, spares and a cooker, we received chocolates, ginger-bread and packets of soup. As usual the letter-reading session was a very blue occasion, prompting much delirious wailing about girlfriends at home. I received the next thousand pages of Proust, much to Dave's annoyance since he could see little reason for lugging such a heavy and unnecessary object across Africa. Steve had now started the first volume so our combined pannier had little room left for clothes. Since the film was no longer a reality, we decided to try and return to Makambako and travel without the trailer. BP agreed to send it further north on one of their trucks, so that we could sell it in Nairobi and raise cash for Christmas.

It felt odd to return to Makambako after a month of malarial festering in Dar. We had never been so far behind schedule and all of us were resolved to tackle a stretch of manic cycling which had become referred to as our escape from Tanzania. We arrived early in the morning and hit the road soon after. Initially I felt fit but fell fast asleep when we stopped for lunch, only to be woken by a ranting policeman prodding me with his truncheon and telling me that I was 'not allowed to sleep'. Severe headaches and cold sweats gave me paranoia about cerebral malaria during the afternoon; thankfully this subsided and I started to shed the stagnation that taints the perception after time spent in a city. Eucalyptus groves and fertile farming land replaced parched black bush and reminded me of Zimbabwe. A twenty-kilometre stretch of straight road passed through a continuous pine forest planted by the Swedes, broken by swampland in the troughs of the undulations. After covering sixty miles, we stopped in Mafinga, where, of all things, we found a jar of Chivers Olde English Marmalade in a shop.

Iringa had always sounded like an intense place – as well as thieves who jump on the back of lorries, we heard that a woman had just been arrested on a bus with twenty human heads in her bag. Voodoo seems to be very much alive in some of these places and we discovered that the area where Chris and Dave had been attacked was quite notorious for its practices. The town is perched above the plains and ribbed mountains stretch their limbs out behind. We were invited to stay with young Irish aid workers who worked for Concern, an exclusively Irish aid organisation operating across East Africa. Dave and I spent the afternoon high on a hill chewing *miraa*, a stimulant stored in the short green stems of a tree, which grows at altitude and is used primarily by Somalians. My head felt vacuous, without being detached, and my vision clear. A soft warming sun showed up the contours below and we came leaping down the hill like mad skiers, feeling vibrantly alert.

Just beyond Iringa the road drops into a steep escarpment; at the top we stopped in a village and watched Dave get molested by an insane old woman with her hands tied behind her back. Using our boots as well as the brakes, we hit high speeds on the descent, suffering two punctures on the way. Narrow winding gorges funneled into a a shaded green gully bordering the Ruaha river; this area was uninhabited and one of the most untarnished we had seen. After ten kilometres we entered a baobab forest which created an unmistakably African feel; some trees were starting to bloom and white trumpet flowers draped from their otherwise bare extremities. As we approached Mbuyuni we saw more and more Masai – young children tending the cattle, wearing beaded jewellery and the proud expressions of warriors.

The following day took us to the edge of Makumi game reserve. The road surface was appalling and we walked through the middle of the day; temperatures were noticeably higher now that we had dropped in altitude and dehydration became a big issue, with Chris throwing up when we stopped to brew some tea. We received more Irish hospitality on arrival at Makuna, feasting on bacon, eggs and beans before settling down to watch a James Bond film on video.

Paranoia about cycling through the game park was dispelled at breakfast when an Irish friend of our hosts offered to drive through with us. It seemed foolish not to accept, especially since he was so adamant, but I could tell that Chris was disappointed at the sense of adventure being reduced. I am quite glad because the first game we saw were lions crossing the road ahead of us. We managed to get quite close and they appeared totally unperturbed by our presence, lethargically wandering off into the long parched grass. The landscape typified my preconception of a game park – savannah stretching to a mountainous background and splattered with acacias sheltering giraffes. Herds of wildebeest were predominant, but we also saw impala, zebra and elephants in the distance. Two menacing buffalos proved the biggest threat, dilating their nostrils aggressively before wagging their tails and turning away. The heat was extreme and rivulets of sweat streamed down our backs.

We rolled on towards Morogoro, watching an ominous storm cloud gather over mountains ahead and dramatic bursts of lightning sporadically shatter the sky, while shafts of light were refracted through clouds behind us and scattered in a fan shape across the horizon; it felt biblical and portentous. Twenty miles short of town we were plagued with eight punctures in quick succession; slow leaks became fast leaks which became big holes. The light faded, we were walking and the mosquitos appeared in profusion. A bedraggled and frustrated TMOAB staggered into the centre of town at about nine. Our contact here was an Irish headmaster called Frank K—, who lived in the Dutch compound, a sealed area of about fifteen houses, originally built by the Dutch but now home to most of the *muzungus* (foreigners) in town. Frank's house was firmly closed up so we barged in somewhere else and explained our predicament. A tall lanky Dutchman with a Gaulish moustache showed us to an area by the pool where we could camp. His name was G.J., he had been in Morogoro for nine years and reckoned he had gone insane as a consequence.

Despite his nihilism he was an amusing and affable character; he took us into town and insisted on buying us roast beef at a wonderful restaurant run by a Mama Pereira. We returned there in the morning for breakfast and got talking to a guy from Bournemouth who was about to catch a lift with a very drunk man drinking brandy. With obvious trepidation he climbed into the car as his driver was carried from the bar, supported under each arm, his lifeless legs dragging along behind. I felt progressively awful during the day, especially after a pustular boil on my arm exploded with green slime.

Frank K— was headmaster of the International School and had been in Africa for three months. The poor bloke seemed to be cracking already and the thought of two more years here was clearly freaking him out; he was totally frantic, smoking like a fiend, trying to avoid drinking gallons of coffee, nursing excessive sunburn all over his body, suffering from stomach trouble and malaria paranoia. He went to the doctor on our first evening, only to be told that he had nervous tension and should take some valium. He was partial to a few tipples every evening and would storm around the house reciting Yeats and Joyce, his mad eyes lolling around his cheeky red schoolboy face. Alternatively he would listen to tapes of Anthony Hopkins reading Dylan Thomas's *Under Milk Wood* and repeat favourite lines with frenzied enthusiasm. He was extremely entertaining and hospitable but not really cut out for his job.

Chris and I were feeling far from normal and went for a malaria test the following morning. Sure enough it was positive and I realised that we had been cycling for at least three days with it flying around our bloodstream. Steve and Dave went for tests as well, found that they were positive also and that evening all four of us were sitting around taking Fansidar and feeling extremely bizarre. For four days we moaned and groaned about feeling insane while mad Frank ranted about 'transmagnificanbandanduality' (a word penned by Joyce) and the Lake Isle of Innisfree. Our favourite distraction was the dictionary game; three of us would give definitions of an obscure word and the fourth player would try to choose the authentic one. Our vocabulary was expanded to include words like 'kismet', 'quisling' and 'slarn'. I found cartons of Gitanes in town and smoked like a maniac over endless cups of coffee. The double-dose of Fansidar, which we had been prescribed, made me feel far worse than the malaria itself and the whole situation felt so ludicrous that we spent most of the day in delirious laughter.

At the end of our recovery Frank persuaded us to go to Dar with him and G.J. to represent the Morogoro darts team in a competition held at the Canadian embassy. We suffered a crazy drive with Frank behind the wheel shouting 'Fock' every time he careered into a pothole, and were installed with Irish friends of his in Dar. We were predictably useless at darts and were out of the tournament in a flash. The rest of the day was spent crucifying our livers by drinking beer, something that should be avoided when being treated with drugs like Fansidar. Chris and I found ourselves battling through waves of nausea and stomach cramps, convinced that if we drank more we would feel better. Steve and Dave pursued a sensible path of abstention. Frank babbled more and more nonsense as he went redder in the face and his bulging eyes threatened to pop from their sockets as he chased girls round a nightclub like a lost puppy dog. G.J. threw up outside and told me he had AIDS.

Steve and I encountered the most offensive man we had met in Africa when we visited immigration in Morogoro to extend our visas. He insisted that it was procedure, *his* procedure, to charge two thousand shillings to extend our permits. Steve adamantly refused to accept this blatant bribery and, after forcing him to admit that he was a bad immigration officer, we left in disgust.

After a delay of ten days we were mobile again. In typically manic style we ended up breaking our distance record on a day we had decided to take easy. The road to Chalinze was as good as any we had seen in Tanzania. From Chalinze north we were expecting it to get steadily worse; G.J. had told us how he had refused to pay the road tax on this stretch in the wet season because the road was not even visible. We embarked on a narrow single-lane road, flanked by lush verges and a variety of vibrant wildflowers; yellow and white butterflies latched onto the bikes before swirling off to the side and shrill birdsong broke the perfect calm. I felt no traces of a malarial aftermath and we ploughed on towards the hundred-mile barrier, falling just short as darkness fell. A passer-by told us about a Christian mission about a mile off the road and we wandered down a muddy hill to see if we could find a bed for the night.

A huge grey colonial building with colourful shrubs along its verandah appeared on a hilltop. We were welcomed by one of two Polish missionaries – a hippie character clad in a floral shirt, who had been here for six years and wanted to stay for 'as long as I can – there is much work to be done.' We were shown to large spartan rooms which Steve likened to a wartime hospital in a French monastery. Dating from 1881, it was the third mission to be built in Africa – this leant weight to my belief that E.S. Grogan must have been here while on his walk through the continent a hundred years ago.

Dave woke Steve and I at dawn and dragged us onto the upstairs verandah. The sky had exploded into a swirling canvas of colour, a dazzling furnace of orange, yellow and red which made Turner look positively tame. Huge billowing expanses of deep orange, a hazy patch of crimson shedding blurred colour like heavy rainfall on the horizon, and thick shafts of light soaring up from behind. We were held spellbound for half an hour as the colours modulated to different hues – deep yellows intensifying and crimsons fading to pinks before merging with an azure backdrop, leaving delicate layers of cloud on a pristine sky.

Banana trees, palms and jungle foliage crept into the bush as we continued due north; the air was humid and insect noises replaced the birdsong. The roadside stalls were covered with tropical fruit, including durians, a foul-smelling but delicious big fruit which resembles a pineapple without the whiskers. It had the taste of a sweet ogen melon and the texture of a banana. A Danish road-building project was setting up its base just beyond Mkata and we pulled in for the night. A crowd of beer-swilling Danes were molesting local whores and guaranteeing themselves a premature death; we slept under a tree, tuned to the drums playing in a nearby village.

Our permits were about to expire and, leaving early in the morning, we had to race to Korogwe for an extension. The immigration officer was the complete antithesis of his counterpart in Morogoro, issuing us with extensions without any mention of a procedure or a fee. Sisal plantations covered open plains and we wound our way through what felt like an enormous painting, motionless puffs of cloud dotting the sky. I was so entranced with Proust by now that I found myself looking at everything through 'his' perspective, certain stretches reminding me of central France and leading me to deliberate over the 'Guermantes' and 'Meseglise' way. I was experiencing the most overpowering feelings of the trip – so much love for the world around me; the spectacular skies, the brilliant flowers, the weird locusts and the delicate butterflies. In the evening, Steve played his most recent song, about a fisherman and an errant soul, leaving me teetering on the edge of tears as rich crimson streaks burnt the sky.

The Usambara mountains flanked the road on our right as we bumped our way along a frustrating stretch – rounded stones lay embedded in the surface, forcing us to weave a path through the thick sand at the sides or even into drainage ditches. Chains kept coming off because the tensions were wrong and we had been too lazy to correct them. We stopped in the middle of the day and spent two hours bashing the bottom brackets with the mole grips, now used purely as a hammer, in a bid to solve the problem. An entire village looked on, intrigued by this unorthodox approach to cycle maintenance.

After travelling another fifty yards a pedal decided to fall apart and dispense ball bearings to the sand. In the next village we were accosted by a babbling old man who claimed that he had seen us in a dream the night before; he directed us up to a sawmill where we stayed the night.

The next leg to Same took us into arid semi-desert. The sense of space was even more pronounced and the scale was calibrated by the regimented cloud patterns receding into the horizon. Over the last few days we had developed an insatiable craving for the fruit which was piled high on stalls in every village. In Same we stood in a circle stuffing ourselves with mangos, oranges and papaya, paying the consequences that afternoon as our previously congested bowels were unleashed with a vengeance. For the first time in months we treated ourselves to single rooms in a guest house; I overdosed on Van and plunged into a vortex of nostalgic melancholy which made me worry about the effect he would have on me once we were home.

I returned from breakfast the following morning to find a chicken nestled into the folds of my sheets like an Arabian princess surrounded by the opulence of a harem; I managed to dismiss my visitor and was left with a freshly laid egg on my bed. Flagrant diarrhoea from our fruit binge had created severe lethargy and we covered the staggering distance of thirty yards in the whole day. The front mountain bike tyre had split so badly that the inner tube protruded in big bubbles and guaranteed constant punctures. We ventured to the town cobbler and watched him stitch in a layer of rubber as Bunny Wailer blared across the market, interrupted by reggae-style Christmas carols. The cobbler's second attempt was successful and we tried to leave. Now we found that the crank on the mountain bike was loose so we decided to stay another night to let our disturbed stomachs settle down in peace. A man called Bavan took us in for tea and told us macabre stories about *juju* medicine involving the genitals taken from small boys.

The owner of the guest house was pleased that we had stayed and said to Dave: 'When does your suffering begin?' As far as we were concerned our suffering had begun long before, and this became another stock phrase for TMOAB banter. The suffering at the moment was a psychological yearning to reach Nairobi – it reminded me of having to struggle through a period of exams. I had never wanted to get somewhere so badly and this anxiety created an irritable atmosphere between us; as usual this was not expressed through arguments but by withdrawing and seeking distraction through isolation.

Information that 'the road from Same is perfect, just like Europe' proved most misleading and kept us amused all day. It could have not been less like Europe and we made slow progress towards Moshi with little sign of tarmac. Quite soon we caught sight of Kilimanjaro surging out of the plains ahead. As we came closer the clouds came down and circled the peak like giant smoke rings. It was a major landmark on the journey and it brought home to me the distance we had covered; I felt a sense of achievement for the first time.

Ten miles short of Moshi we were pulled over by two French firemen in a Peugeot estate who were part of a three-vehicle expedition taking medical supplies to Rwanda. As we talked the other vehicles appeared, old red ambulance vans with sirens. It was the first time that we had encountered any transport that looked more surreal in the middle of Africa than the trandem. In Moshi we went straight to BP to collect the trailer and unanimously decided that we did not want to pull fifty kilogrammes of unnecessary weight one mile further. Fortunately a tanker was going on to Arusha the following day and agreed to take it for us.

Steve, Dave and I were feeling pathetic. The thought of more malaria was too much to bear and we quaffed industrial quantities of glucose over breakfast to try and get motivated. After ten miles of masochism my strength returned. More and more Masai appeared, looking utterly stupefied by the trandem as they tended their cattle and goats on the arid plains. Broken spokes on the freewheel side delayed us during the middle of the day, which was actually quite a relief, giving us all time to recharge our dwindling energies. A downpour drained the humidity from the air as we approached Arusha and the feel of rain on my face accentuated the masochistic drive which was propelling us all towards Nairobi. We co-ordinated free passage for the trailer up to the border, had an argument with the manageress of the Greenlands Guest House after she refused to give us a room we knew she had, before finding rooms in what was undoubtedly a brothel. Our appetites had disappeared now and we mashed up some avocados in a bid to ingest some food.

The road out of Arusha climbs steadily up several miles before levelling into beautiful green pasture amidst rolling hills; without the Masai kraals it would look like the Cotswolds. We had our first successful photo session with the Masai, managing to get them in shot without their demanding money. Dave was visibly wasting away; he had lost an unbelievable amount of weight in the last few days so he continued at his own pace on the mountain bike. A straight gradual descent took us down to a dry hot plain. The heat created a mirage to our right – a lake of placid water with a group of four Masai running in formation across the surface. There were no habitations and there was no water until Longido, a small settlement sheltering under a peak in the distance. I had never been so thirsty and the last ten miles was the most taxing cycle we had experienced. On arrival we wandered about in a detached delirium, making stupid noises and laughing at our decrepit condition. The only sustenance we could find were a few stale chapatis which cracked like dry wafers and made us feel even more dejected. With only twenty-six kilometres separating us from the Kenyan border, we soon grew restless and charged on. Tanzania bade us farewell with a torrential rainstorm but nothing now was going to prevent us from completing our escape.

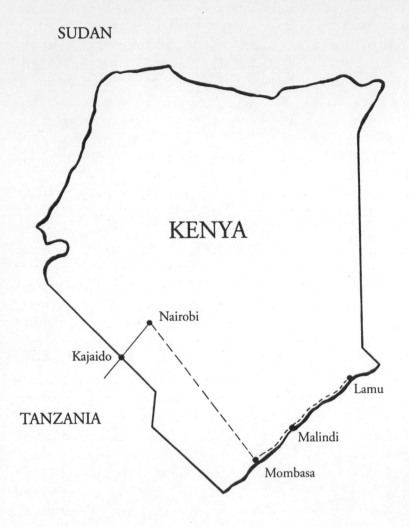

SUDAN

KENYA

Nairobi

Kajaido

Lamu

TANZANIA

Malindi

Mombasa

0 — 200M

APPROX. SCALE

Kenya

Two Kenyan hustlers adopted us before we had even passed through immigration. Both were chewing *miraa*, vigorously chomping their jaws and insisting that we change our remaining Tanzanian shillings with their friend. For once we tried to change some money officially. At the River Hotel the manager agreed on the transaction only if we promised to eat dinner and breakfast there, so we returned to the hustlers. They were now 'whizzing' like mad, talking incessantly at the same time, instantly reminding me of Cheech and Chong movies. While we ate they made frantic calculations over the bill, jabbering like Pinky and Perky on speed. The taller one was a Samburu called Abdullah Lengis; he poured forth about tribal customs, his spiel garbled but interesting. The shorter one was a Masai called Kashmiri which seemed incongruous in itself; he spoke less English but kept telling us that his father had eleven wives and over fifty children. After a few beers we walked into the bush for a smoke; Kashmiri kept leaping about and doing press-ups while Abdullah told us about his LSD experience in Nairobi when he dropped a tab and went to see Arnold Schwarzenegger in *Commando*. Back at the Guest House we were entertained by an old Masai guard – after removing several layers of clothing and pumping up the hurricane lamp for maximum effect, he demonstrated the Masais' distinctive pogo dance for us.

Cheech and Chong reappeared at breakfast, the day's chewing already under way. It was overcast and a humid drizzle filled the air. The road took us through lush pastures and the crest of one hill gave us another view of Kilimanjaro. Steve felt his fourth bout of malaria brewing and went for a blood test on arrival in Kajaido. There was little surprise to learn that he was positive again and even he found it impossible not to laugh at the absurdity of his misfortune. With only forty-eight miles between us and Nairobi, Steve decided he had to cycle. The dull rain made a pleasant change from the clear skies and searing heat of Tanzania.

Finally finding Nairobi in our sights was an extraordinary feeling; I kept thinking about staring at the maps in London and how we had tried to envisage what we were now experiencing. The reality was, as always, very different from the mental image I had nurtured in the back of my mind for months.

After Athi River, a drab truck-stop town where we attended to more broken spokes on the freewheel side, the road merged with a dual carriageway for the last stretch into Nairobi. Adrenalin mounted as the skyscrapers signifying the centre of town appeared on the horizon. It prompted thoughts about the approach we would make into London, our ultimate destination. Time always plays weird tricks in these situations and the last ten miles felt more like thirty. Excitement, combined with tension and fatigue, exploded into an untimely confrontation between Dave and I when we fell off the trandem half-way round a roundabout. It required some determination on both parts to dispel a sour aftermath before reaching the Thorntree Hotel for celebrations.

The strangest thing about our arrival was, suddenly, for the first time, seeing more white people around us than black. They struck me as clean, tidy and boring; self-absorbed, restrained, confined by the insular limits of their conservatism and completely removed from real life. We took a perverse delight in shocking all the tourists assembled in the café sipping their cups of tea, by immediately ordering a bottle of champagne. One American woman had nearly fainted when we drew up on the trandem and wandered in, uttering a terrified 'Oh my Gawd'. We did look extraordinary, Steve on the verge of collapse and all of us festering in filthy tattered rags. The incident made me aware of our own reality and how difficult it seemed to communicate with any of these people who spoke our language.

Within an hour of our arrival, having persuaded the equipment manager to put another bottle on his Visa card, Mamba Dowling appeared. He took us off to Ma Roche's Guest House, a mecca for

overlanders in Nairobi, before taking us off 'for a bit of a feed and
some piss' in the evening. It was hard to fathom whether he had been
north, south, east or west in the interim but here he was, the same
as ever, hanging out in Nairobi and patronising the infamous Green
Bar which was open twenty-four hours a day.

Chris and Steve were installed with friends of Chris's parents. Dave
and I found ourselves with a friend of his mother's called Frank S—,
suffering the company of two English girls who thought they were
seeing the world; their three-month stint in Kenya had taken them no
further than the Watamo Ocean Sports Centre. Frank's wife had died
two years before and he struck me as a lonely, lost soul, anxious to be
with young people, drinking excessively and eating hardly at all. He
was laid back and one felt no sense of social pressure in his house. On
our second day he took us for a very odd, liquid lunch at the Turaco
Club, which was full of brown clothes, beer and gossip. Meanwhile
Chris and Steve were enjoying the comforts of a beautiful house about
a mile down the road. Mr and Mrs S— were incredibly hospitable,
immediately offering us the run of their house over Christmas. He
was one of the last great game hunters, organising trips up north
for that international market of people who love killing things. His
wife was open-minded, relaxed and perceptive, giving us free rein
over a vast library of paperbacks. She made arrangements for us to
meet 'some young' on the second night and Dave and I made our
way over. She seemed to have made quite a hasty assessment of us
because we were introduced to the most decadent group of 'young'
she could have mustered.

Somehow we were invited to a very smart drinks party held by
a Danish family. Predictably we were the last to leave. I had been
enthralled by the grandmother, an incredible woman in her eighties
who recounted outrageous stories about a wedding she had attended
in the Sixties where the cake had been laced with hashish. When we
finally left the house after midnight, she looked like she was ready
to start partying.

After ruling out the possibility of cycling through southern Sudan,
Somalia or Ethiopia due to omnipresent war zones, and having
toyed with the idea of taking a boat to Djibouti, we realised that

the only option for the road ahead was to fly on to Khartoum as originally planned; the sponsorship money from Chloride in Kenya would just about cover the flights. Our applications for Sudanese visas went in as quickly as possible; we were told that it would take two weeks to process them and we could pick them up in early January. We tried to tie up as many jobs as possible before the Christmas break, exchanging spares, selling the trailer, visiting AMREF and co-ordinating publicity for Chloride. Rob Bertram, the MD in Kenya, did everything within his powers to make our stay in Kenya as luxurious as possible. He arranged for us to stay in the Chloride apartment in one of Nairobi's finest hotels, lent us a car and gave us free use of the telephone, something he regretted after Chris spoke at length to his girlfriend in Australia.

The crazed friend in London, who had sent the tape of Krishna chants to Malawi, had always threatened to join us in Kenya at Christmas. Accustomed to his mad antics, we had never known whether to take him seriously or not. Then, one day, we received a message: 'Colonel Kurtz is coming in low'. He was on his way. Christmas immediately took on a different atmosphere – unspeakable derangement was sure to follow. One afternoon we were sitting in the Chloride apartment when a bearded, grinning apparition came tumbling over the railings and onto our balcony; Organ had arrived. It was strange to see a familiar face after eight months but we clicked immediately and the madness poured forth. Organ regaled us with stories about the 'summer of love' which had occurred in our absence and we soon realised how pervasive the house scene had become. We still had jobs to do in town and for a few days he roamed the streets trying to arrange deals; within three days he had been ripped off to such a degree that he had no money left. However, he had made the foolish mistake of bringing his Visa card.

Steve's girlfriend Emily flew out to join him over Christmas. They disappeared north to Lake Naivasha, and would meet us for New Year's Eve in Lamu. Two days before Christmas the rest of us boarded the train to Mombasa, clutching huge bundles of *miraa*. We shared our compartment with a Somali man, who was a *miraa* connoisseur and proceeded to chew his way through a large bag. He claimed to manage one of the smart hotels in Mombasa but I could not quite equate these wired, frenzied eyes with someone in a position of such responsibility. We talked at each other throughout the night, arriving in Mombasa with gooseberry eyes. After waiting around in the centre of town for Organ to get ripped off a bit more, we boarded a bus for Malindi, where we planned to stay the night before moving on north to Lamu. Malindi beach was a massive disappointment – polluted, crammed with horrendous hotels, full of equally horrendous people. While setting up camp, the equipment manager, always the first person to reprimand others for not guarding their valuables, had his money belt stolen. This was the end, not only of his passport, Visa card and traveller's cheques, but also of the entire Christmas party fund, which had been carefully accumulated over previous weeks. We knew exactly who it was – a group of young children who had been lurking nearby – and a very boring saga developed, culminating in a confrontation with one boy's father. Needless to say the money never reappeared and we arrived in Lamu the following day with enough cash to rent rooms for three days and no other access to money other than Organ's Visa card.

Lamu is an island. There are no roads and no vehicles. It has a predominantly Muslim community and has been regarded as the second Mecca. The old town is made up of tall, white-washed houses, intersected by narrow alleyways fanning out from a central market place. The sweet smell of frankincense billows onto the streets, mingling with the thick aroma of strong coffee which is constantly brewing in dimly lit stalls. Donkeys provide the only form of transport and the sight of fully grown men hurtling round corners on the poor creatures is both alarming and comical.

On arrival at the quay we were latched onto by Charlie, one of Lamu's leading hustlers, who could be spotted at any time of day or night striding purposefully through the sinuous streets, his hat adorned with flowers and a handful of *miraa* driving him on towards the next intake of scrounged stimulants. The house he took us to proved perfect – a three-storey palace lived in by the sultan of Lamu in the eighteenth century. We were installed on the ground floor, which incorporated one huge room with kitchen facilities and a large dining table, with two adjoining bedrooms and a bathroom. The main room became a time vortex where, like Blairhall, hours and minutes passed in a disproportionate manner. A central courtyard provided the only access for daylight, which splashed down onto tall, waif-like papayas. Two raised areas in the central section of the courtyard provided altars for burning copious quantities of frankincense. Although the white-washed walls could have benefited from some restoration, the original Islamic mouldings were still intact, creating large three-dimensional patterns on all the flat surfaces. Two huge black wooden doors, beautifully engraved and sagging with age, swung laboriously open to reveal the main bedroom – a long, narrow room, with one wall covered in archways, receding a few inches into the thick stone, and stacked on top of one another like miniature tombs. The black timbers of the roof were interrupted at intervals by larger beams, decorated with small magenta motifs.

A steep staircase took one from the main entrance up to the middle floor, which was occupied by a variety of different people throughout our stay, including an elderly American teacher from Uganda, who entertained a steady stream of Lamu rent-boys. I first spoke to him in the market place late one night, while watching a group of young men stamp-dancing and singing harmonies. I had romantic visions of him being a celebrated author working on his latest masterpiece in Lamu, but was disappointed to discover that he was really rather dull.

A very narrow stair took one up to the roof, made extremely perilous at times by water discharged from the shower, cascading down to the drain at the foot of the steps. The roof circled the central atrium and also provided space for four small rooms. A low white-washed wall and thick timber rail skirted the edges and prevented fools like us from plummeting to the ground. The view from one side receded into central Lamu across flat roofs – some left bare, others covered by a low thatch over tables and chairs. The other side looked towards the sea-front and had a dominating position over much lower houses. The view was slightly marred in the day by the dockside crane, but by night it had transmuted to another weird shape. A few tall palms tottered above nearby houses, constantly rustling in a gentle sea breeze. Two chairs proved ideal for star-gazing and one became referred to as the space chair due to the angle at which one was forced to sit, precluding one from conversation and jettisoning your vision towards the heavens; bats would swoop across the sky, momentarily mistaken for shooting stars; during the day fish eagles flew between the vantage points of the crane, a TV aerial and the palms, occasionally soaring higher and gliding in great sweeping circles. At night my attention was always grabbed by a fan-shaped light thrown up behind some palms onto the flat wall of a big house on the sea-front like an enormous screen.

Over Christmas we spent a lot of time on the roof with Bob, a Canadian who had been cycling through Europe, Turkey and parts of Africa, and Brennen, an English guy from Rochester who was about to return home after five and half years on the road. Bob was short and squat with flowing fair hair and a moustache; he looked like one of The Eagles. Brennen was covered in jewellery, had a short, bristling beard and short hair, with one long plait hanging down the back like a rip cord. He had been working in South Africa and then started travelling back overland to the UK – three years ago. He had worked in Zimbabwe, Malawi and Uganda, usually as a DJ, and certainly had a story or two to tell. We were also joined at this time by Kevin, an Irishman in his late thirties, who had been travelling for twelve years. He had spent a lot of time in India and seemed well entrenched in the Goa scene. He liked to talk about his exploits with the local talent wherever he was and revealed that in Muslim countries he makes them keep their veil on.

Christmas Day started late in the morning with a few beers and plenty of smokes. Consequently very little happened until the mid-afternoon when we somehow managed to pull our heads together and start preparing the gastronomic feast. The liquid remnants of a very fragrant stilton, which my mother had sent me for Christmas, was whipped into a rich sauce for some lobsters. Brennen attempted, rather unsuccessfully, to make mayonnaise; Chris laboriously peeled two kilos of prawns and Organ applied himself to making gallons of tea from a stockpile of *miraa*. We sat down to eat as the sun sank and a vibrant glow shone through the clouds of incense. A haphazard game of charades was attempted after the meal, before staggering to the disco at the police canteen.

Shelah, the main beach on Lamu, is about forty minutes' walk from the town. It costs a few pence and takes ten minutes to travel to by dhow but due to our lack of cash we found ourselves walking. The only place that took a Visa card was Peponi's Hotel, situated at the near end of the beach; consequently it was the only place where we could eat, drink or buy cigarettes. Every morning we would saunter in, order a beer each and buy a packet of cigarettes; on every occasion we would decide that, since this only amounted to about two pounds sterling, it was too meagre to warrant using a credit card and immediately order a second beer; this in turn led to a third and, before Organ had a chance to say otherwise, we would book ourselves in for lunch.

Peponi's is a discreet white-washed flat-roofed building with a strong Mediterranean feel. It was built in the Thirties and has been run as an exclusive hotel since the Sixties. The current owners are two brothers, Neils and Lars, who took over the management from their father and seem to have maintained the hotel's unique atmosphere. A pergola smothered in bougainvillea serves as an outdoor restaurant, and variegated tropical shrubs mingle with rustling palms to enhance the exotic ambience of a seemingly unpretentious hotel which makes no attempt to advertise itself. A stream of jet-setters passed through over Christmas and New Year, pushing us to further excesses at the peril of Organ's Visa card.

We returned to Nairobi, distinctly disabled by our Christmas break. Sanity seeped back after Organ's departure and we busied ourselves with the dilemma of progressing north. Our Sudanese visas were showing no sign of materialising, and once we heard that UN officials were having difficulty in securing theirs, due to developments after *Sharia* (Islamic Law) had been officially imposed by the Muslim government in Khartoum, we decided that radical alternatives must be pursued. These ranged from heading through the war zones in Somalia and Ethiopia, to flying west to Agadez and cycling up through the Sahara, or flying straight to Cairo and cycling up and down the Nile until we had clocked up a distance equivalent to what we had missed out. After a few days of trudging between embassies, my severe animosity for cities resurfaced, especially for Nairobi, and I felt uncontrollable urges to escape. Before Christmas, in a futile bid to sell the remaining 16 mm film stock, I had met Damien Bell, who lives with his mother Carol in a beautiful house on the edge of Nairobi game park. I rang up and they invited us to camp in their garden at the bottom of the gorge, which forms the boundary with the game park.

A fast-flowing stream bubbled over some rocks into a wide pool where it slowed to an almost stagnant calm. A large moulded black rock sat in the water like an organic bronze sculpture, consequently referred to as the Henry Moore. The area was currently ruled by a group of big, bad baboons and the first two days were spent trying to define the new territorial limits. Steve was insistent that we should pee over all the surrounding bushes, a tactic which he reconsidered after a huge male baboon chased him up a tree in pursuit of the mango he was eating. A series of intense staring matches from the Henry Moore helped to establish who was allowed where, and after the second day we were left in peace.

Overhanging the stream, on our side, was a tall tree with a series of three platforms which had been built as a tree-house for Carol's youngest son. For some reason I was obsessed with the idea of sleeping on the top platform, about forty feet up, and on the first night I climbed up with a torch, my volume of Proust and my sleeping bag. The platform was triangular and about four feet across at the wider end; this was clearly where my head should be I thought. On my right a thick branch would prevent me crashing to mother earth. However, on my left, there was nothing but a vertical drop towards Steve and the tent below. I placed my thick volume on the edge, convinced that if I did roll in that direction it would act as an adequate barrier and save me from a broken neck. Happy with my safety precautions, I slid delicately into my sleeping bag and lay down to sleep. During the day the gorge was totally tranquil – birdsong and the soft lull of cascading water was all that could be heard. At dusk the fireflies appeared, like a silent warning of the cacophony to come. Just as I lay down to sleep, it started – one loud belch from the other side of the stream triggered off another and then another until at least a hundred bullfrogs were croaking to each other across the gorge, the confines of which amplified the noise to a near deafening level. They continued incessantly into the night and faded only with the first signs of dawn. I was getting accustomed to the frogs when the baboons decided to join in and a few appeared in the branches below me. Sleep was looking more unlikely by the minute and when a hyena joined the party I ruled it out completely. For about two hours I stared directly at its luminous yellow eyes, not sure whether I was provoking or deterring it; finally, just before dawn, it lost interest and I fell asleep.

Sleep came more easily on my second night up the tree, and by the third I had controlled my paranoia to a manageable level. It was a strange, almost masochistic desire to push levels of fear which had driven me up there in the first place and it became a special place with a special perspective associated with it. I started to spend most of the day up there as well, reading and writing as the sun fell through the leaves, creating dancing, dappled patterns on the paper.

This was a clean-living and creative period for both of us; Steve continued to write great songs and great poems while I wrote pages of introspective drivel, tried to meditate and purge my system of toxins accumulated over Christmas. By the time we left, I felt that I had glimpsed a tiny part of a wholeness that we all ultimately strive for; I felt like I was part of what lay around me; I felt balanced and complete. I had also written the first poem that I have ever felt proud of – a feeling which lasted all of five minutes.

Like a river in full flood,
After years of withering drought,
Nature now flows in my blood,
And drives stagnation out.

Euphoric energy waves,
Surge and fall inside;
My enraptured soul now bathes
In this relentless ebbing tide.

Our visas finally appeared on February 7th, my birthday. Flights were fixed for the 10th and we prepared for the unknown quantity of Sudan. Leaving the gorge was weird; I really felt that I was leaving part of my self behind. Some lilac flowers sprawling across a boulder on the other side of the stream and which closed up every day before dusk, seemed to wave goodbye as I looked back over my shoulder.

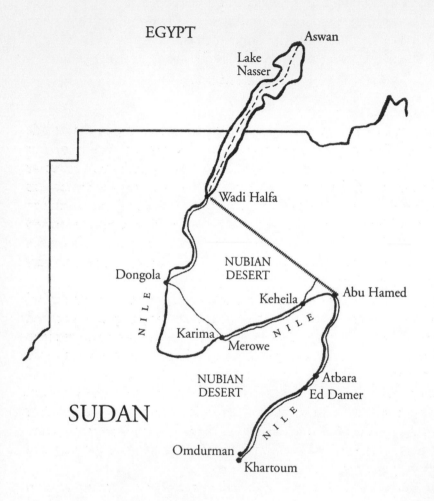

EGYPT

Aswan

Lake
Nasser

Wadi Halfa

NUBIAN
DESERT

Dongola

Keheila

Abu Hamed

NILE

Karima

NILE

Merowe

NUBIAN
DESERT

Atbara

Ed Damer

SUDAN

NILE

Omdurman

Khartoum

0 — 200M

APPROX. SCALE

Sudan

According to astrologers we had chosen the worst day of the decade to travel. The lunar eclipse started at the exact moment of our departure to the airport and shrouded Nairobi in black velvet as we sat silently in the back of a Chloride van like convicted prisoners on death row. We had developed an image of Sudan from talking to people in Nairobi; African people tend to present a very distorted view of their neighbours, so we knew that 'a few mud huts by the Nile and thousands of starving people' would hardly be an accurate description of Khartoum.

In fact central Khartoum appears to be a prosperous and beautiful place – a rare combination. Well-fed businessmen, elegantly swathed in pristine white robes and turbans, could be seen disappearing into air-conditioned offices and using fax machines. An avenue shaded by sycamore runs alongside the Nile, and the imposing colonial buildings have gained a serenity and charm in their deterioration. The further one travelled from the centre, however, the sadder it became – long, wide boulevards with dusty, dirty sidewalks, flanked by rows of half-constructed concrete houses, looking like an apocalyptic film-set.

As was customary with our arrival in a city, we dithered around for two hours trying to formulate a plan of action. This involved the painful process of persuading Dave to ring one of his contacts. While Dave tried various telephone numbers at The Meridien Hotel reception, we were approached by two shifty hustlers. 'Cockney or Limey?' one of them asked. I opted for Limey and they gave me a quick run-down on black market rates, cash or travellers' cheques, and offered me every narcotic I have ever heard of. Having only spent about two hours in a country where hanging is mandatory for any black market activity, let alone drugs, I decided that dealing with these guys would be particularly foolish.

The contact we had been given in Khartoum was Osama Latif – the head of Sutrac, the Sudanese Tractor Company – and one of the most influential bigwigs in town. Osama's hospitality was almost embarrassing, especially since we looked like tramps. We were adopted by a large and ungainly old man from Sutrac called Ebrahim, who treated us like his own sons and kept us amused with an inexhaustible repertoire of ancient folk tales about the beauty of Sudanese women. He ushered us around town, and with the utmost tact and charm placed us at the front of every queue.

Having spent six weeks trying to obtain our visas to get into Khartoum, it was mildly frustrating to learn that we needed another permit to leave. What was intended to be a twenty-four hour stay was immediately prolonged to at least a week. We were paraded in and out of various offices like stuffed exhibits, while Ebrahim diplomatically overcame the disdainful looks of Immigration officials and senior policemen. We never uttered a word in any of these meetings, just shuffled around conscious of our dire appearance.

The route ahead was far from settled. We were well aware that the tarmac terminated about thirty kilometres north of Khartoum and that for the remaining three hundred and fifty kilometres to Atbara we would be following tracks in the sand. For some unknown reason we imagined this stretch to be the least of our problems, probably because it looked like a relatively good road on the Michelin map, marked with a thick red dotted line. From Atbara things looked more dubious; we were down to a thin yellow line as far as Abu Hamed, on the edge of the Nubian desert. From Abu Hamed a rather ominous purple line ran parallel to the railway line across three hundred and seventy kilometres of desert to Wadi Halfa. Apparently two masochistic Germans had struggled along the railway line on mountain bikes and arrived in Atbara thoroughly dejected and very thirsty. Bumping along over railway sleepers for three hundred and seventy kilometres was clearly out of the question for the trandem. The only other option was to continue beside the

Nile – some semblance of a track did appear to trickle out of Abu Hamed in the form of a very small dotted black line, but even this disappeared into a great quagmire of yellow.

We tried to gather as much information as possible about the terrain in various places. This proved to be pointless – people either told us we were mad or that there was nothing but sand. Nevertheless, the stretch across the Nubian was intriguing – we were convinced that it must be possible, especially after hearing that there were two stations with water half-way across. However, that still meant carrying water for four of us for about one hundred and eighty kilometres, which was completely out of the question. Then one of us had the bright idea of 'doing the Nubian on a railway trolley'; the theory was that we could carry as much food and water as necessary and 'whip across the desert'. At least we would still be on man-powered transport and would not be 'cheating' on trucks or trains. This was generally agreed to be the ultimate solution to our problems and Ebrahim took enormous delight in arranging an audience with Mr Frejoun, head of the Northern Regional Railways.

Mr Frejoun was to be found lurking in a dank, dusty office in a labyrinth of corridors overlooking the central station. The entire railway network was built when Sudan was under British rule at the start of the century, and little has been updated since. We stood in silence while Ebrahim set to work with habitual enthusiasm. Mr Frejoun looked increasingly bemused as he grappled to understand why four Englishmen should want to borrow a railway trolley. Eventually he turned towards us.

'How long will it take you to reach Atbara?'

'Well, let's see – it's about three hundred kilometres, so a hundred kilometres a day, so about three days – so we should be there this Sunday.'

'I will be in Atbara on Sunday, so come and see me there and we'll see what we can do.'

This was all that was needed to convince us that all problems had been overcome and that we would be laughing all the way to Egypt. Our travel permits would be ready for collection the next day, we could leave the following morning and reach Atbara on Sunday, leaving ample time to complete the stretch to Wadi Halfa. What deluded fools we were.

Our state of dress had degenerated to desperate levels. We looked like a bunch of penniless vagrants and were totally unequipped for the freezing temperatures of the desert at night. The cheapest and most effective way to smarten our appearance was to buy a Sudanese *galabiyya* each; it would also double the layers of clothing at our disposal.

The market crowd was kept amused for half an hour as we tried to choose our *galabiyyas*. I eventually settled on the cheapest option, the classic no-nonsense cut which had a subtle purple tinge in the white. To complete the image I insisted on having a turban, for which I sacrificed my last T-shirt. On our way back we were befriended by a restaurant boss on the corner of the market who offered us a free breakfast if we came back in the morning.

We were sleeping on the floor of a courier company office called AEI, managed by Osama Osaka, a friend of Osama Latif's. He took us, clad in our *galabiyyas*, to the Sudan Club on our last evening. The Sudan Club is the last outpost of a faded past – housed in an impressive building, slowly receding into obscurity. While signing the visitors' book, a red-faced colonial type walked in behind us.

'Anybody seen Tubby Greaves recently?' he boomed at the doorman.

A bar which must have once resounded with colonial cocktail parties, it is now spartan and austere, serving only lemon juice to an eclectic mixture of aid workers, embassy staff and selected local residents. While Osama played squash with Chris, in bare feet and a *galabiyya*, we relaxed on the verandah with our lemon juice, trying quite hard to look like Lawrence of Arabia.

About seven the next morning we returned to the market with the bikes loaded up. The owner of the restaurant, who seemed to hold sway over the whole market produced an enormous bowl of *ful* (beans) with raw onion, tomato and felafels, keeping the swelling crowd of children at arm's length from the bikes. I reluctantly agreed with the others that maybe I did need a pair of shoes – and bought 'the desert clogs', a remarkably uncomfortable pair of rigid leather shoes which, within two days, had created huge festering abscesses in my heels. I persevered with them for two weeks, wearing them only when circumstances dictated, until I realised that the damage done to my feet by wearing them was far greater than what I would have suffered without them. In a fit of frustration I hurled them into the desert near El Kirbekan, but retained septic sores on my feet for the next three months to remind me of them.

Riding through the outskirts of Khartoum that morning was one of the most disturbing sights of the year. The relative prosperity and elegance of central Khartoum gave way to a sprawling wasteland – a smouldering rubbish tip stretching for miles, and home to hundreds of thousands. Tiny shelters, made from old sacks draped over a framework of sticks, provided most of the housing. Some were luckier, owning a sheet of polythene or even corrugated iron. Death, decay and toxic fumes filled the atmosphere. We watched a dustbin lorry empty its contents before a gathering of people, fighting to find something for their livelihood – a scrap of clothing for one of their children, a piece of material for their home, or best of all, something to eat.

Thirty kilometres north of Khartoum the tarmac did come to an abrupt halt. A network of tangled tyre tracks unwound themselves over the next few miles, before finding their own course across the desert. As we discovered, it is quite easy to lose sight of these tracks. We also discovered that it is quite easy to lose all sense of direction. We had been told that it would be quite straightforward – 'Keep the Nile on your left and the railway on your right and you'll find yourselves in Atbara'. I am sure that in a four-wheel drive vehicle this is very sound advice, but when your means of transport restricts you to twenty-five miles per day, it is rather vague.

A group of fly-infested stalls marked the transition from tarmac to sand. There was a depressing atmosphere and little to eat – some ancient *ful* and unripe guavas served up by mongrel children with aboriginal features and wild matted hair. After following the tracks for a few miles we found ourselves shooting across a vast flat gravel plain, shrieking with laughter. Tearing aimlessly across that plateau was a huge release, a sudden liberation from all the delays and frustrations of the last few weeks. It felt refreshing to leave the congestion and mindless bureaucracy of the city behind, and once again to be united with nature, this time in her barest and simplest form – the desert. The sheer volume of space immediately felt therapeutic, a great void in which to off-load mounting tensions and frustrations.

Meanwhile the railway disappeared on a tangent to the right and the Nile became obscured by a long ridge on the left. The hard gravel plain turned to long stretches of soft sand and we were walking. We were also lost. The fertile, inhabited band by the Nile had long since disappeared and telegraph poles marking the railway were just discernible in the east. We consulted the relevant map from the collection we had obtained from the Survey Department in Khartoum. These maps were part of a 1933 survey, made by a Corporal Bradcock, and they seemed to mark virtually every tree and boulder between Khartoum and the Egyptian border. We decided that we were near to somewhere or something called Abu Zibil, that the Nile had disappeared into Sabaloka Gorge and that it would only take an hour to reach the river if we headed directly for the end of the ridge. What looked like two or three miles must have been closer to ten because as dusk descended we were still floundering in the wilderness, our initial excitement had waned and anxieties were mounting.

The clarity of desert light is similar to that at high altitude, enhancing the vibrancy of colours against the sand. However, in mid-afternoon the western horizon was obliterated by white light, draining all colour and definition of distance to our rear. The ridge ahead revealed more of its features as this harsh light turned soft and golden, transforming the pale brown to a rich terracotta. A small gathering of mud houses appeared just as we started to worry about our lack of water; women and children were ushered inside as we approached, but feelings of trepidation dissolved into hysterical laughter as soon as we changed into our *galabiyyas* – 'Aaaaah, Sudan *galabiyya*, koiss?' ('Koiss' is the Arabic for 'good' and it punctuated our conversation for the next few weeks.) We were immediately presented with chai which disappeared down parched throats and

prompted more mutterings of 'koiss, koiss'. I had never felt so dry
– hair, skin, eyes, everything coated in a film of powdery dust. A
splash of water on my hands and face only partially removed this
sensation, draining off my skin like water on polythene.

We were shown to a small empty room; rickety rope beds and a
bowl of deep red plum tomatoes materialised from other houses. We
cooked some of our pasta over a charcoal fire, mixed in tomatoes and
garlic, and shared it amongst the assembled party. Steve strummed as
the pink glow of day receded and the chill of night descended. Little
communication was possible since our grasp of Arabic at this stage
was limited to the one word; between us we must have said 'koiss'
a thousand times that evening.

Sleep is light in nomad camps; I was woken up several times
during the night by the brightness of the moon, as if somebody kept
switching a bedside lamp on in my face. The sun started to warm
the desert as we made another attempt at lightening our load. This
was always a frustrating exercise; what seemed totally superfluous
to one person would be of critical importance to another. Somehow
Steve's harmonica holder remained – the ultimate unnecessary piece
of equipment for any discerning expeditioner, it was used three times
throughout the year. We discarded spare brake blocks, agreeing
that brakes were fairly redundant now that we were reduced to
walking through sand all day. The medical kit became even smaller
and we presented a pile of potions to our delighted hosts; Chris
then spent an agonising half-hour using sign language to persuade
them not to swallow bottles of chloroquine every time they had a
headache.

An endless stream of chai appeared from every household – sweet,
spiced and frothing with fresh goat's milk. I pondered over Corporal
Bradcock's map and tried to ascertain where we were. I read out
several place-names but received very blank expressions in return.
Only Abu Zibil seemed to provoke a response; they all pointed to
the middle of the ridge ahead and announced 'Abu Zibil' in unison.

Vaguely relieved by this information, we thanked them with our
expanding Arabic vocabulary and set off. Distances continued to
be deceptive. Our initial estimates proved to be way out because

at midday we were still stumbling across a huge expanse of black boulders. Early morning eagerness had long since subsided, water bottles were empty and conversation limited. By two we had walked over twelve miles and ridden about four hundred yards. The only signs of life were some melon-shaped balls growing on creepers that sprawled across the ground. The Nile was still obscured and the heat transformed the horizon into a shimmering lake. Eventually we came within a mile of the ridge and a small blob, possibly a house, appeared to our left – Abu Zibil, we assumed. The small blob slowly revealed itself as a nomadic kraal, a cluster of three shelters made from dry twisted branches.

Two old women appeared, their furrowed features cracking like dried clay. They clearly thought it strange to be walking bicycles across the desert in the mad dog, but dismissed it as a European eccentricity and offered us some water. An old man on a donkey emerged from the distance; he greeted us and then withdrew, watching intently as we cooked a current speciality – a packet of pasta with several cloves of fried garlic. I tried again to establish where we were. 'Abu Zibil?' I asked confidently. Nothing; just an inquisitive stare, so I tried again. 'Abu Zibil?' I tried several times, placing different emphasis on different syllables; still nothing. For two minutes I said nothing except 'Abu Zibil' until I had tried every permutation of pronounciation. This seemed only to bewilder them further; we thanked them and continued our stumble across terrain covered in boulders.

After stubbing my toe ten times on ten different rocks, we reached another gathering of more permanent shelters. A few thorn acacias had appeared, shedding black pools of shadow onto the sand like oil slicks. We made a small fire using camel dung and brewed up some tea amidst a mass of children. Meanwhile two teenage boys plodded in on camels, bearing lush green animal fodder; the river must be close now we thought.

The remaining five miles to Sabaloka and the sanctity of the Nile took us through the softest sand so far; for the last half-mile this turned to gravel and allowed us our only ride of the day. Drawing up beside the first people we saw, we asked where we could buy food. One of them spoke a little English and insisted that we ate at his house; apparently *ful* was not available but there was *kiseran*. *Kiseran* was to become our staple diet for the next few weeks; on this occasion it was very thin, like a crepe, and served with what can only be described as a green splurge, called *mula*; apparently it is an extract of okra but it has the unappetising consistency of uncooked egg white. At the time it was utterly delicious and the whole bowl was whipped down in seconds. *Kiseran* could also be served in thick layers, like lasagna, with tomato and onion, or even thicker like a stodgy pancake.

Most of the houses were situated about half a mile from the river because of the frequent floods which burst over the banks every year. We rode down past the green wheat fields for our first swim in the Nile. The fertile irrigated fields were a welcome sight after two days deprived of green, and the contact with water felt almost like an alien sensation. Inevitably we were besieged by a crowd of curious children, laughing hysterically at us as we washed on some rocks by the bank. I retreated behind some reeds to write my diary.

The atmosphere of the place was almost Biblical – arid ravines and parched colours; the profusion of donkeys and camels; long-flowing white robes and turbans; the sweet smell of frankincense on the banks of the river Nile. The complete lack of modernisation – no tarmac or modern building materials – added a timeless quality; there was absolutely nothing to tell you which century it was.

This tranquillity was marred by the disappearance of a camera film. Donkeys kicked fine powdery dust into the air to create a sombre evening haze as we wandered back to the village. Whilst deciding on a place to camp we were once again ushered into an enclosed courtyard and presented with the most beautiful meal – five different dishes, arranged around a pile of *kiseran* on a huge circular steel plate. A deliciously spiced potato dish was particularly memorable.

The overwhelming generosity of these people is difficult to describe; it is so spontaneous and selfless. This was to become more pronounced as we travelled into remoter areas. If we had accepted every invitation for tea or food we would quite literally still be there;

it became commonplace to have five invitations to eat breakfast before nine in the morning. People would wave from where they were working in the fields and then implore you to come and eat with them; it felt more embarrassing to refuse than accept. We tried to repay this boundless hospitality but offering money in return was the ultimate insult. Sometimes we would try and slip notes under plates to be discovered later, or try and offer something from our belongings. The problem was that we were now carrying so little that we could not afford to lose anything (Steve's harmonica holder was hardly a suitable gift). The lasting impression from the whole year, which will stay with me forever, is of all the people in northern Sudan who gave us absolutely everything within their means. I wish that we could have done more for them.

In view of our lack of progress over the last two days, we decided never to lose sight of the Nile again. Walking was still the norm, following tracks along the edge of the fertile band that separated us from the river. This band of green was never more than half a mile wide and could not have been more of a contrast to the desolate view on our right. We passed through an almost continuous stream of linear villages, the distance to the next always distinguishable by the minaret of a mosque. Bands of wild young gypsy girls would stare intently from their donkeys as we passed, their colourful clothes and dreadlocked hair giving them a mysterious and romantic attraction.

We paused in the market town of Hagar el Asal for mid-morning *ful*. The market consisted of a series of concentric circles, partitioned into separate stalls. Eager to seize the chance of spending some money, we dug into an enamel bowl of beans. However, when we tried to pay, the owner of the restaurant refused to take any money. This was becoming too much and we insisted on buying him tea from the adjoining stall. Meanwhile a conspicuous character with western dress, glasses and an afro hairstyle had wandered in. He spoke good English and started interrogating us. What were we doing here? Why had we taken photographs of the mosque? Realising that he suspected us of spying, we tactfully explained that spies do not travel through deserts on three-seater bicycles, and that there was not a great deal to spy on in the desert anyway. He left us in peace.

In the next village I realised that my stomach was seriously congested with several meals of *ful* and *kiseran*. We were in the centre of town, surrounded by most of the male population, and I needed the loo very badly indeed. It also happened that none of them spoke a word of English; or so it seemed. Whilst trying to exercise severe restraint, clenching every muscle in my behind, I reeled off every English word for loo that I could think off – no response except puzzled faces and laughter. Dave tried to rescue me with an explicit charade, squatting on the ground; this purely provoked more laughter. Just when I thought every blood vessel in my head was about to explode, Dave added audible groans and a pained expression to his increasingly graphic charade.

Immediately one of them said, 'Aaaaah! WC?'

'Yes, yes, WC,' I stammered, before being whisked off through a courtyard to the nearest hole in the ground.

On the fourth day the railway reappeared on our right while we were struggling through some mud by a burst irrigation ditch. By following the railway we would at least know that we were heading north in a straight line, rather than randomly following paths round ridges, villages and fields. After pulling the bikes through a mile of sand, it was a relief to find that the surface between the tracks was hard enough to ride on. All hard surfaces in the desert turn soft sooner or later – something we should have learnt by now – and within ten minutes we had resumed our walk. We followed the railway most of the way to Atbara, occasionally cycling, occasionally running and pulling the trandem, but usually walking.

Turban-tying techniques seem to express a powerful sense of individuality. Sitting in a tea and coffee shop in Kabushiya, surrounded by about twenty old men, I noticed that every turban was slightly different – some were meticulously coiled into a spiral of taut rope, looking serious and austere; others were swathed in an elaborate but haphazard twirl with about eighteen inches draped down the back, crowning a romantic dignified face with a perfectly groomed conquistador moustache. Entering the cafés often felt like stepping into an Old Master painting – the crumbling texture of the walls in the soft light; large, battered cooking vessels over charcoal fires, tended by parched, leather faces under white skull caps. On this occasion Steve was lumbered with the village idiot, a quivering, emaciated character who looked like he had chewed too much nicotine for his frail frame to cope with.

The Meroe pyramids are just north of Kabushiya on an escarpment, about one mile east of the railway. They enticed us with their pagan attraction and we decided to make a detour to sleep there that night. The closer we came, the less dramatic they appeared. However, a resounding primeval silence and a sense of ancient majesty pervaded the place. A low fence enclosed them and large signs from the Ministry of Antiquities made it very clear that sleeping there was strictly illegal. While we were deciding where to jump over the fence, an old man in skiing sunglasses appeared from nowhere carrying a leather satchel. From this he produced sheets of official paper with official stamps and official signatures; these made little impact on us because they were all written in official Arabic. Anyway, he seemed to be the official guide because he had keys to all the restored tombs. The pyramids were miniature compared to what we would see in Egypt, had all lost their peaks to plundering European 'archaeologists', but were covered in beautifully preserved hieroglyphic carvings. Sadly our official guide did not speak a word of English so we learnt absolutely nothing about them, except that this was the main burial ground for the kings of the Meroetic Kingdom, which spread throughout this area between 300 BC and 400 AD.

When we returned to the bikes we found a line of ten children sitting cross-legged on the ground; displayed in front of them were old knives in leather scabbards, little clay pots and jugs, leather *dawa** parcels containing pages from the Koran and the head and neck of a large bird – one boy insisted on opening the long beak and shoving it in my face while making bizarre squeaking noises. I felt no desire to own the tattered remnants of a bird, but I did buy a small leather *dawa* from a beautiful girl with pigtails.

For the last stretch to Atbara we were advised to take the desert road used by the trucks. It was apparently straight, flat and hard.

---

* A little leather charm containing a page of the Koran

Momentarily forgetting our vow never to leave the river again, we embarked on the most intense desert stagger so far. The first few miles were indeed no problem, we actually sat on a bicycle seat for a change. Soon the flat plain became a series of undulating ridges and the troughs in between started to fill up with soft sand. This continued for a few miles and then levelled into a flat gravel plain again. However, what appeared to be a hard surface was too brittle to support the weight of the trandem and we just sank every time we tried to ride. Once again it was the mad dog, we were walking and we had no water. The plateau was on a slight curve and the horizons on every side seemed to drop away off the edge of the world. The heat created vast mirages of placid water up ahead. It was the bleakest landscape imaginable, a different planet. It was also furiously hot. The only natural feature to break this monotony was a small outcrop of rounded red rock, which further convinced me that we were on Mars. Beyond this we found a series of red and white poles marking a recently laid gravel road which disappeared into the mirage ahead. Convinced that this must lead all the way to Atbara, we leapt on the bikes with sighs of relief. Within a mile this mysterious road and its markers came to grief. The view ahead was bleaker than ever – nothing. We agreed that it was the weirdest road ever and resumed our walk.

An hour later a few black marks broke the level horizon. Rarely have I wanted to get somewhere so badly and never has anywhere so obstinately refused to come closer. It was another hour before we could identify these marks as buildings, and two hours later we tottered into Ed Damer, a small town just south of Atbara.

A very embarrassing scene developed on arrival. We walked into the market to find several mounds of enormous watermelons. I decided that there was nothing in the world that I wanted more than a watermelon, but I refused to believe that one could cost twenty Sudanese pounds, the equivalent of ten meals in a restaurant.

'Twenty pounds?' I shrieked. 'No way – I'll give you five.'

'No, no. Twenty pounds.'

As there were several piles dotted around with different vendors, I thought I would waste no more time and try someone else. He also quoted twenty pounds, as did all the others; this convinced me that they were all in league against me and I got angry. I felt totally tormented, standing in front of hundreds of water melons after walking for several hours through the desert with no water, and absolutely refusing to pay what I *knew* to be the wrong price. Then one of them gave me one for free. This threw me completely. Making an awkward apology, I gave him twenty pounds, which he now refused to take. This was too much and I disappeared in disgrace. The following day I discovered that the authentic price for a watermelon was indeed twenty pounds.

While in Kharthoum we had been allowed access to the Pickwick Club, a 'legal' drinking club attached to the British Embassy, which draws a steady influx of British nationals every afternoon. It was here that we met Howard Borsden, the only person we spoke to who could give us any detailed information about the route ahead, insisting that the most beautiful and interesting part of northern Sudan was between Dongola and Halfa. He was based in Atbara, running an agricultural project, and his parting words were: 'My name is Howard – when you reach Atbara just ask for me – everybody knows me.'

So, here we were in Atbara, riding towards the market, asking every passer-by if they knew Howard. Nobody did, and we descended on a tea shop to enjoy *shishas* and *kakady* for the first time. A *shisha* is a water pipe, through which you smoke bowls of perfumed moist tobacco; *kakady* is a hot drink made from hibiscus, which is the colour of Ribena and supposedly lowers your heart-rate. The *shisha* delivered a furious nicotine rush to my brain, leaving me half-asleep, while the *kakady* reduced my pulse to an alarmingly faint tremor. I could hardly move for an hour, let alone find Howard.

We did eventually find Howard; he drove past in his Land Rover while we were lethargically wandering the streets. His house was hidden behind a high wall near the market and had a small enclosed courtyard. He lived with his wife and another relief worker called Brian, who immediately produced pints of beer, home-brewed with his kit from Boots. We told Howard about our plan to continue on a railway trolley and he suggested talking to Peter Bridges, the head of the Canadian Pacific's Railway Rehabilitation Programme. After some dinner, Howard drove Chris and I to the old colonial club where we found about twenty Canadian Pacific Railway representatives sitting on the verandah, drinking lime juice but wishing it was gin and tonic. Peter Bridges was a frail, balding man in his late forties who would have looked more at home in a monastery than here in Atbara trying to restructure an obsolete railway network. We looked like escaped lunatics – barefoot, draped in *galabiyyas* and crowned with dusty dreadlocks. He told us that Mr Frejoun was leaving for Khartoum in literally five minutes; if we raced to his house we might just catch him, bearing in mind that no train leaves on schedule. Of course this proved to be the exception – Frejoun's train had miraculously pulled out on time. We went on to what was supposedly his house, but instead found a collection of very forward and enticing student girls who had just moved into their digs. Howard dragged us away.

The next morning we all assembled in Peter Bridges' office. He was struggling to fully understand what we were up to and what he should do about it, so we managed to dictate the course of action. Frejoun must be contacted in Khartoum to give authorisation for our request; we could proceed from there. We reappeared before lunch and, much to our surprise, discovered that contact had been made, authorisation had been given, and a trolley would be put at our disposal. This fortunately stalled any brewing plans to try and cycle across the Bayuda Desert – a hostile expanse of sand, stretching to the west. At two o'clock we collected a very unofficial-looking piece of torn scrap paper covered in Arabic, which we were to present at every station to get a trolley for the next stage of the journey. Every station has its own trolley, so it was deemed impossible for us to take the same trolley the whole way. This had all been dealt with by Mohammed Abdullah, a large, jovial character with a genial smile and Dennis Healey eyebrows.

Atbara market extends over a series of intersecting dusty streets on a grid pattern. The shops sit under a crumbling colonnade that runs the length of the street, constructed from blue steel pillars. The meat market sits in the centre, where thousands of flies obscured the carcasses. Rows of herb and spice stalls sold everything from frankincense to fennel and cinnamon, piled high in circular steel buckets. Aubergines, carrots, marrows and greens covered the stalls, as well as the ubiquitous tomatoes and onions, beside buckets of dried dates, dried chillies and dried okra. Young boys polished shoes; old men diligently operated their Singer sewing machines. Hopeful traders were selling everything that ever fell off the back of a lorry: keyrings, dodgy digital watches and plastic combs. Coffee, chai and *shisha* stalls were on every corner, always full of men consuming caffeine and tobacco in every conceivable form – in *shishas*, rolled into cigarettes or suffused through the gums from a ball of tobacco delicately placed under the lower lip. Dave became quite partial to this. The first time I tried, it was a disaster – within seconds I had little pieces of tobacco stuck in every part of my mouth, creating a very unpleasant burning followed by a tremendous urge to throw up. I spent about ten minutes spitting little pieces of tobacco from the deeper recesses of my mouth. The next time I was extremely careful and found that once you had the technique, it could be a very satisfying buzz. Cigarettes were in short supply because of war rations and we gradually became quite addicted to this unattractive habit. The only other nicotine option available was a rolling mull from Chad called *Gumsha*. We never deduced exactly what constituted *Gumsha* but there seemed to be a high proportion of green leaf involved.

I was arrested for taking photographs in Atbara market. Once again I escaped further interrogation by asking the policemen who would send spies to the deserts of Sudan on a 1930s trandem.

Feeling exhausted from a lack of sleep, I motivated myself for the cycle to Berber, where we were to pick up our trolley. It was a particularly unpleasant ride, despite being on reasonable roads; a strong headwind made progress painfully slow, and we had to contend with the worst dust storm so far. Steve started feeling very weak which prompted fears of more malaria.

We arrived in Berber to find all the restaurants closed and more policemen wanting to inspect our papers. During this tiresome routine we were approached by an Old Testament figure wearing an olive-green *galabiyya* and clutching a staff. We were led back to his house for lunch where we found ourselves surrounded by the most prominent members of the community. A morning prayer session was in full swing; ten elderly men sat poised over copies of the Koran, fiddling with prayer beads. They were all well-educated and spoke excellent English; one of them had been at London University and had cultivated a very large plum in his mouth. Although anxious to discuss religious beliefs, especially the similarities between Islam and Christianity, they remained dogmatic in their views, unable to acknowledge a difference in belief due to cultural or geographical circumstances.

Leaving Steve asleep, we made our way to the station and presented the station master with our official note. This did not have the desired effect. It transpired that we only had permission to take a trolley from Abu Hamed to Karima or Wadi Halfa. Amidst huge aggravation and flaring tempers, we hung around for several hours while they tried to contact Atbara on a telephone which I could not believe would operate, a tangled confusion of wires which spewed over the crumbling plaster. However, contact was made and the truth reaffirmed, which was doubly frustrating since we had explicitly agreed with Mohammed Abdullah that we could pick up the trolley in Berber. The idea of returning to Atbara at this stage seemed horrific; especially with Steve feeling ill and the time running out on our visas. Eventually we calmed down and agreed to take the train to Abu Hamed that evening; at least it would give us more time to tackle the final stretch.

Steve started feeling stronger, and we prepared ourselves for the train. Just before we left, the younger men in the family ushered us to the back of the house and into a room full of women, ranging from grandmothers down to baby girls. It was an embarrassing situation as we tried to strike up conversation amidst a barrage of giggles. Our departure was prolonged by a deluge of requests for shampoo and skin cream; unfortunately we could not oblige but I doubted that this was the real reason for our visit.

At the station we were plagued by a very drunk station master who took a peculiar fancy to Dave and insisted on calling him 'my dear'. He also insisted on weighing both bikes on scales no bigger than a wheel. Obviously this was a pointless exercise and we left

Dave to try and explain that our bicycles were too big to fit on the machine.

'But my dear, you must weigh the bicycles . . .'

The train clattered in at ten, only two hours late. Suddenly it was chaos as we ran down the carriages looking for space; every door we opened revealed a seething mass of people. The roof was the only option as the whistle blew and we shunted off. Meanwhile Chris, anxious that the station master was now in possession of the bikes, had disappeared. Before we had travelled a hundred yards it was evident that we had made a big mistake – the jolting motion threatened to throw us off the side every five seconds and it was very, very cold. We tentatively started to roll out our sleeping bags and put on the sum total of our clothes; this was far from easy as the roof was only five feet wide and curved. Eventually I was installed inside my 'sleeping beauty' and lying across the roof; seconds later I was slipping off the side and grappling for something to hold on to. I handcuffed myself to a metal pipe with a pannier strap through my wooden bangle and reassured myself that it would save me if I fell off. (The metal was so cold that bare skin actually stuck to it anyway.) What I had failed to account for was the howling blast of cold wind which now inflated my sleeping bag like a parachute and created conditions akin to a deep freeze. I pulled the top of the bag over my head and resigned myself to a twelve-hour nightmare. The only other people on the roof were two scantily clad locals huddled under a small blanket; quite how they survived I will never know. When the sun rose I looked up to see Chris two carriages behind, tied to a similar pipe with his belt. We congregated at the end of our carriage and pretended that it was getting warmer; the icy wind was still biting into exposed skin but all we could do was laugh.

Abu Hamed reminded me of a small town in a spaghetti western; low, white-washed houses and a pervading sense of lethargy. Looking rather pathetic, we shuffled into the market and deposited ourselves in the first restaurant. A large bowl of *ful* was a welcome sight but was marred by the little rocks that seemed to be a principle ingredient in this stall's recipe. Several glasses of tea and coffee were needed to help the digestion, before returning to the station to try at last to secure the trolley. For once our piece of paper seemed to serve its purpose – we could collect the trolley in the morning and start our journey. We set about buying provisions from the only *dukan* (shop) in town – choice was limited and we left with packets of pasta, biscuits and two kilos of halva. We also splashed out on little triangles of processed cheese, which were all eaten by that evening, and some powdered orange concentrate called *Tang*, which was very nasty but did transform brown salty water into something more refreshing.

The trolley saga entered yet another phase the following morning. We were summoned to the radio room after breakfast to find two senior officials who confirmed that we could take a trolley from here to the first station in the desert, Station Number Ten, but that there would be no trolley there to continue with. Once again we hovered around while they tried to contact Atbara on antiquated radio equipment and once again we received new information – we must be accompanied by a Sudanese railway employee. We also discovered that the officials in Atbara wanted us to take the goods train that left that evening for Karima; clearly they were fed up with the whole escapade but we persisted, explaining that we were not here to take trains and that we must speak to Atbara ourselves.

'Oh no – they're having breakfast.'

'When will they finish breakfast?'

'One hour.'

One hour later we returned to find a very deserted station except for one man lurking in the radio room.

'Can we try Atbara now?'

'Not possible.'

'Why?'

'No electricity.'

'When will there be electricity again?'

'Maybe tomorrow.'

'*Maybe* tomorrow?'

After a period of resigning ourselves to the idea of another train journey and despairing in the futility of the whole venture, we discovered three redundant trolleys under a tree. Two were too dilapidated to consider taking anywhere but we lifted the third onto the rails and started pumping our way up and down the stretch of track in front of the station.

'Nothing wrong with this,' was the verdict.

This bizarre spectacle had attracted an audience and one of the railway workers offered to find some grease. We set to work brushing a thick crust of dirt off the moving parts and revealed a small plaque: 'Made in Sheffield 1926'. At least it was a contemporary of the Goodloid's. The grease did not appear for a few hours and we retreated to various corners of the station, mumbled about having bilharzia and went to sleep. In the late afternoon we slapped generous amounts of grease onto the wheels, axles and gear cogs and tried again. With four of us pumping the bar we managed a reasonable speed and felt confident that this was the most practical way to be crossing the desert. While following the railway south of Atbara we had met an oncoming trolley with four workers on board. We reckoned that they were doing 'at least twenty kilometres an hour'. Hence it was quite alarming to be told in Abu Hamed that it took at least four hours to reach Station Number Ten, which indicated an average speed of five kilometres per hour. We chose to ignore this information, arrogantly assuming that our fitness would make us faster.

The next morning we went in search of the elusive chief engineer who still had to give us permission to take this trolley. He was in midstream on the switchboard and after a short wait we waded in with our request. His negative response threw us into tantrums, issuing wild ultimatums about letters to Frejoun in Khartoum. This did little to help and we sulked off to the market. While trying to find a restaurant that did not serve little rocks in its *ful*, we were approached by a man in western clothes who had witnessed our despair in the radio room. He explained that he actually worked for the Post Office but wanted to try and help us out; apparently he had secured permission for us to take the trolley as far as the third station where we would transfer to another. We were then invited to share breakfast with him and his friend, who produced a large block of feta cheese and broke it into the *ful*.

We returned to the station and started loading up the trolley like a gypsy caravan – both bicycles lashed precariously to the front, threatening to fall off and be chewed up by the cast-iron undercarriage; panniers, water bottles and boxes of food tied to the central support and the guitar lying across the top. This left enough room for the four of us to stand and operate the bar. We were all set to leave when the problem of our 'accomplice' was mentioned again. It was tempting to race off before they could produce someone foolish enough to come with us, but they claimed that he had gone to have breakfast at his house and would be with us in half an hour. After an hour we asked again. This time he refused to come with us unless we paid him four hundred Sudanese pounds. We knew that his weekly wage was forty so we offered him sixty for what would be a maximum of four days' work. This seemed like a fair deal to the assembled crowd but he still refused to have anything to do with us. Patience was at a threshold and I withdrew to write.

By midday the situation was resolved; we were to be accompanied by not one but *two* people. Nobody was going to argue any further and, true to form, we set off in the mad dog sun, confronted with three hundred and fifty kilometres of desert. It was evident before we lost sight of town that this was going to be considerably harder work than we had ever envisaged. We found ourselves grinding uphill into a headwind, carrying a few hundred kilos of bicycles, equipment and unnecessary passengers. Half-way to the first station I decided that this approximated to my conception of pure hell more accurately than anything I had ever had the misfortune to experience. The trolley that we had so hastily deemed to be 'absolutely fine' in Abu Hamed was actually on its last legs. The big gear cog was failing to engage on the drive wheel for half of each revolution, producing an unbearable grinding noise on the downward stroke. On the upward stroke all you could see was the sweating pained expression of the person opposite, bursting with exertion as the sun drained every limb of the liquid we so desperately needed. The physical commitment made it impossible to hold a conversation. Instead we suffered the inane banter of our companions, who insisted on fondling each other, wailing Sudanese folk songs and stopping us every few kilometres to roll cigarettes for them.

We soon found that we travelled faster and with less effort by taking it in turns to walk behind and sulkily kick the back of the trolley forward. It took nearly five hours to cover the twenty-three kilometres to the first station, by which time we had considered every conceivable alternative. Rested, we decided to persevere to the third station, where we hoped to find a slightly more operational trolley. A pure sunset shed a therapeutic effect on TMOAB: the new silver sickle moon was hanging directly above, while the sky radiated bands of diffused colour, culminating in a deep burning orange which covered the western horizon. Such pure and intense colours in such silent space; no dramatic cloud, just the vivid clarity of the desert set ablaze.

The next morning we made much better progress with the wind behind us and we were spared pushing the trolley most of the way. Initial energies soon faded, and we found ourselves back in Vulcan's Forge pumping iron in a blistering furnace, restraining ourselves from knocking our two companions off the side and leaving them stranded in the wilderness. The older one spoke some English phrases, which he insisted on repeating incessantly and then spelling out letter by letter. This was broken up by frequent reminders of 'Karima very far'. He insisted on demolishing vast quantities of our dwindling tobacco supply by dispensing the majority of it to the wind in his efforts to roll cigarettes. Whenever we hit a downhill they would join in with an exasperating chorus of 'Ooooh! Aaaaah!' This provoked us so much that we actually travelled faster, unleashing our exasperation on the bar.

Keheila is a small village clinging to the Nile, seeking refuge from the encroaching dunes. Surrounded by palms and fields of green wheat, it was a beautiful sight after two days of sand as we cruised downhill into the station. The trolley intended for the next leg was parked nearby; by now we were so exhausted and fed up with trolleys that we overlooked it and headed straight for the shop, where I started talking to the local schoolmaster, who looked just the part with his high forehead and receding fuzzy hair. He told me that a road ran along the other side of the river to Karima. None of our maps marked a road anywhere in this area so I pressed him for more details. It was apparently quite hilly, but hard enough to be used by the lorries which appeared every other week to deliver provisions and take produce to the market in Karima.

This part of the Nile was more dramatic than further upstream; the steep clay banks, which are cultivated at this time of year, dropped a hundred feet to the water. Since the rains had failed the previous year, the river was very low, revealing long muddy sandbanks whose rounded forms ran up and down the river. Rocky crags projected like dorsal fins, parting the flow of water. A young girl, with thick black matted hair and a vibrant red dress, looked on as we swam. I walked the length of the nearest sandbank, my eyes glued to the intricate patterns in the black sandy clay which formed great twisting arabesques, their forms highlighted by the deposits of white sand in each trough. The turquoise in the water intensified in the twilight, while a silver line lapped against the shoreline like a trail of mercury. Impulsively I wanted to ditch the trolley and plunge into the most isolated area we would come across; the idea of three more days in the desert without any glimpse of the Nile, no fuel to cook with and having to endure the unmitigated nightmare of the trolley, all combined to convince me of this alternative. We would remain by the Nile, see the fourth cataract and be surrounded by mellow people all the way to Karima. Dave's pragmatism could not quite grasp this, and the rest of the evening was spent trying to rationalise every piece of information into a satisfactory argument. Chris and I were adamant about this decision, Dave was 'not convinced' and Steve 'just didn't know anymore'.

We had been befriended by Abdulbagi, a young man who had been at agricultural college in Dongola and now worked a farm in Keheila. He insisted on bringing us dinner from his house in a stack of stainless steel pots – *kiseran*, tomato and onion salad and some *mula*. We explained our new plan and he offered to take us across the river in his boat if we came to his house in the morning.

I withdrew into the dunes to meditate. I concentrated on the Sanskrit syllable 'Om', the eternal hum of the universe which Hindus and Buddhists believe signifies the sound of creation. I repeated the sound as I sank into meditation and, for the first time, heard it reverberate within me and through the air around me. I felt light and lucid, hardly able to sleep under the bright night desert sky.

"   In the morning we walked to Abdulbagi's house, where we found him building an extension with huge bricks of dried clay. His family insisted that we ate breakfast with them before we set off. Five minutes later, Abdulbagi appeared in the central courtyard, bearing a lamb in his arms; innocently he asked Steve if he liked eating sheep. Unaware of the implications, Steve replied that he did and within two minutes the unfortunate animal was hanging off a pole in front of us, being skinned. Embarrassed by the extent of their hospitality, I wandered outside to take some photographs and on my way back looked into the kitchen to see the women and children squabbling over the raw entrails. Nearly one hour later we were seated around the biggest banquet of a breakfast imaginable: inexhaustible mounds of *kiseran*, salads, spaghetti and bowls of stewed lamb meat. By the time we had been allowed to stop, and were physically incapable of eating more, we found that we were almost too bloated to move.

Lethargically we wandered down to the river and loaded the bikes, panniers and guitar onto a very small boat. This left little room for the four of us plus Abdulbagi and a friend, so Chris and I volunteered to go swimming. There was a long sandbank about halfway across and we walked upstream of it to ensure that the current did not carry us past. Halfway to the sandbank I realised that the current was considerably stronger than we had supposed; I also remembered how much we had just eaten and immediately started to feel very heavy, envisaging myself sailing over the fourth cataract, frantically waving my arms.

We narrowly escaped being swept past the sandbank, where we stopped to get our breath. Meanwhile we could see the boat, totally out of control, disappearing downstream towards some rocks. The second stage of our swim was across a longer stretch of faster water and we found ourselves washed up half a mile downstream from where we had started. During this time the boat had run aground on rocks, broken an oar in an attempt to avoid them, and was now rotating its way downstream. We could just see Steve nervously holding his guitar while Dave frantically issued instructions to the helpless oarsmen. Fortunately nothing was lost and five minutes later we were all assembled on the far bank.

The road was hard and beautiful, surrounded by black shale. It weaved its way up, over and round the undulations, through small cuttings and gorges, across dry riverbeds, over irrigation channels and past the fluttering baize wheat-fields. The top of a ridge would reveal a small Bethlehem below, nestled into the folds of the rock formations; the crumbling fudge buildings merged into the landscape, sometimes only discernible by their cubist shapes being given form by the contrasting light and shadow. Sometimes the villages would seem hauntingly silent, deserted like a ghost town, sometimes derelict and burnt as if in the aftermath of a battle. In others were men, women and children working amidst the silver sheen that the breeze blew across the wheat, men of all ages riding or driving donkeys, sometimes in procession to the next village, or laden with water splashing out of sagging rubber saddlebags. The only disruption came from the ubiquitous diesel water pumps, the lifeline of the whole area.

I felt weaker and weaker throughout the day. By the time we stopped to camp by the Nile I could not even muster the strength for a swim. Shivering from dehydration I lay down in my sleeping bag and watched the sunset. For the next two hours I depressed myself with hepatitis paranoia to such a degree that I actually felt relieved to find that I had dysentery. The people in this area were the most timid and apprehensive that we encountered; they watched from a distance as we gathered dung for a fire and then they disappeared into their houses. It was a peaceful spot and I spent the night staring at the swaying dusty palm trees silhouetted against the sky.

The next day we found that this road, like so many others, had the annoying tendency to disappear into the desert for indeterminable distances. Consequently we resorted to the donkey track – a narrow, sinuous path that rambled through small ravines, between huge boulders of black rock and across the continuous network of irrigation channels and sand-swamped *wadis*. This led to some of the most manic cycling to date on the mountain bike and the most strenuous work with the trandem. We hit plenty of soft sand, averaged about fifteen miles of walking and one mile of cycling per day, and ate lots of *kiseran*.

One morning, while ambling through a village, I was hit by a waft of my favourite smell – fresh coriander, which was growing beside an orange grove. As I stood savouring this we were invited to eat breakfast by three men sitting nearby, making a bed by winding brightly coloured rope around a metal frame. It was one of the most memorable breakfasts of my life – sweetened scrambled egg, tomato and onion salad, yoghurt with honey and small cups of strong coffee, all arranged on a circular plate under a colourful, woven lid. Halfway through this one of them produced a beautifully drawn map, marking every hill and village between here and Karima, the donkey track and the lorry route. Dave immediately fell in love with the map and never let it out of his possession after I managed to rip it the next day. Just before leaving I was approached by a man who had been staring curiously at the trandem while we ate breakfast.

'Petrol, yes?' he asked.

'Petrol, no,' I replied.

This seemed to cause great confusion and he asked me the same question again. I spent five minutes trying to persuade him that the trandem had no engine and did not need petrol. This clearly made little impression because as we left he was still muttering, 'Petrol, yes?'

Feelings of a different world in space and time had developed. 'How far to Karima?' we asked in one village. After a quick consultation between various elders we were told: 'One hundred kilo'. The day before it had been 'eighty kilo'. Karima and El Kirbekan continued to get further away the closer we came, until I was greeted at El Kirbekan by an enthusiastic schoolteacher who was quite adamant that Karima was 'more than one thousand miles'.

While enjoying a rare stretch of cycling one afternoon, we came over the crest of a ridge and tried to gather as much momentum as we could to take us as far as possible through the sand at the bottom. We ploughed into the sand at about twenty miles per hour, stopped dead in our tracks and all flew off the side of the bike. The front wheel had hit a boulder hidden under the surface and was now buckled beyond recognition. After standing around for ten minutes making stupid remarks, we sat down under a sad, spindly piece of scrub, which provided the only visible shade and started trying to reconstruct a wheel. We were confident at the outset that we had everything we needed – spare rims, spokes and hubs. However, it transpired that our hub was for forty-eight spokes and the rims were only for thirty-six. Convinced that this was a surmountable problem, we set Steve to work. One hour later we were still staring at an empty rim, having tried every mathematical permutation possible. Our only option was to put the mountain bike wheel on the trandem and take it in turns to carry the mountain bike. This soon got referred to as 'the yoke' because the most comfortable way to carry it was with one's head through the frame. We took it in two-mile bursts and walked through several small villages looking more incongruous and bizarre than ever. While suffering my second stint of the yoke, I prayed that we would meet someone who spoke English and knew of a truck leaving for Karima the following day. After walking over ten miles, we entered a lush green basin, stretching up towards us from the Nile. About a mile up we could see a large settlement and decided to stop there for the night. Formations of small birds swooped over the ripening golden wheat as we approached and I reflected that although this stretch of one journey had ended in disaster, we had passed through the most isolated and beautiful region yet. I consoled myself that ten miles of the yoke beside the Nile was infinitely more mellow than ten miles of the trolley in the middle of the Nubian. Just then we were spotted by some men in the fields to our right and one of them came running up to greet us.

'Have you come to see the fourth cataract?' he inquired, in Oxbridge English.

'No – I am afraid we have a problem with our bicycle,' I said, pointing to the buckled wheel, 'and we must get to Karima as soon as possible.'

'There is a lorry in the morning going to Karima.'

'Thank God.'

Sadly this was the end of our cycling and walking in Sudan. By the time we reached Karima we only had three days in which to leave the country before our visas expired. We were tempted to risk staying longer but the idea of failing to complete the journey within the year because we were rotting in a Sudanese jail made us think again. Even by lorry we only just made it. The journey from Karima to Dongola in the middle of the night was unforgettable. I was poised over the cab, freezing in my beauty with the broken zip and forced to concentrate on the surface lit by the headlights, bracing myself at every bump to prevent myself being hurled forward and run over by our insane driver. At one stage I moved to the back in an attempt to find more space. I found an old man huddled in a twelve-inch gap between two crates. Every time we hit a bump, which was every ten seconds, both crates would crash down against him; I am surprised that he survived. I tried prostrating myself on a crate over the rear wheels and wound as many ropes as possible round my arms and legs – I spent the next hour trying to induce blood circulation back in to my hands and feet. I spent another hour kneeling at the back, clinging onto ropes and pretending I was in a rodeo; this was fun for five minutes but desperately intense thereafter. I must have chewed several ounces of tobacco that miserable night, unable to roll any *gumsha* in the Siberian gale whistling around my ears. When we arrived at Karima in the early hours of the morning I tried to warm my insides with endless cups of strong coffee. The caffeine and nicotine mixture left me so strung out that for the whole day I could hardly speak.

The next leg to Kerma was considerably more comfortable, despite having to squat on a barrel the whole way, which sent me reeling from side to side like a clown in a circus act. The final stretch to Wadi Halfa we did by bus, expecting it to be more comfortable than a truck. In fact it was like being in a boxing match; after every stop the driver would sound the horn and it was like 'seconds away, round five' as one spent every second until the next stop trying to dodge another blow from the sharp metal corners protruding all around. We were poised over the rear wheels, clinging to a metal bar on the seat in front and performing gymnastic manoeuvres as we hit another bump at full speed and got launched towards the metal luggage racks above. If your concentration lapsed for a few seconds you were in trouble; your head would crash against the metal above, knees would crumple against the seat in front and then the base of your spine would receive a powerful jolt as you landed back in the seat – all within a split second. To make matters worse the driver decided to demolish most of a bottle of *araki* at one stop. We went tearing out of town like bats out of hell and it became one of the most terrifying trips of my life as the driver launched flat-out into the night, taking every corner sideways. I was quite relieved that the other passengers were equally concerned but every plea for him to go slower only incited him further. At about two in the morning there was a loud bang and the bus slewed sideways to the edge of the road as I saw remnants of a rear tyre flying through the air. I looked out of my window to see the driver literally fall out of the cab into the sand; he did not move until daybreak, clearly too spun out to deal with the situation. Meanwhile everybody else got out of the bus and fell asleep beside the road.

Reaching Wadi Halfa was quite a relief and arrangements for the boat to Aswan were helped considerably by Osama's cousin. We found some space on deck, under the lifeboats, and watched the soft pink of evening fall across the water. As the horn sounded and we pulled out from the quay, I suddenly felt uncontrollably sad – somehow aware that I was leaving Africa here.

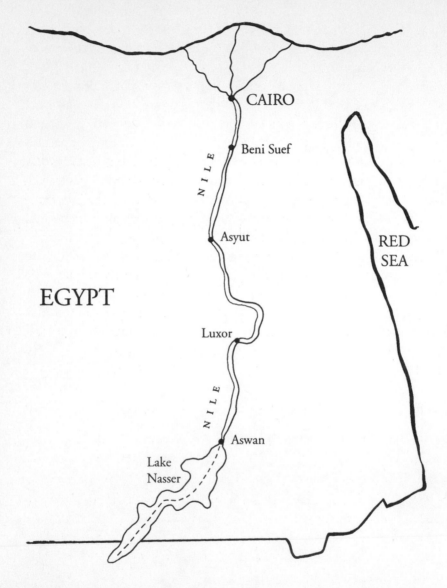

MEDITERRANEAN

CAIRO

Beni Suef

NILE

Asyut

EGYPT

Luxor

NILE

Aswan

Lake
Nasser

RED
SEA

SUDAN

O — 100M
APPROX. SCALE

Egypt

My sadness upon leaving Halfa was not unfounded – arrival at Aswan felt like landing in Europe. A concrete blob of a building housed customs, immigration and duty-free shops full of hoovers and fridges. Smooth asphalt took us past rows of squalid and decaying modern apartment blocks before depositing us on what felt like the French Riviera – monstrous boats teeming with anaemic Europeans sporting fashionable swimwear, a promenade where the tourists outnumbered the locals by five to one and Parisian style cafés with tables and chairs outside and green wooden shutters above. It combined to make me feel displaced and estranged, reawakening the loathing I had felt for complacent white society on arrival in Nairobi. Watching tourists wander past, overladen with video cameras and casting disapproving looks in every direction, could not have offered a more marked contrast to the beauty, purity and humility of the Sudanese.

A visit to Elephantine Island with Chris was the one redeeming feature of our arrival in Egypt; it was situated in the middle of the Nile, less than a hundred yards from the rows of tourist barges, and evoked a wonderful sense of relief as we wandered along dusty, winding paths, under groves of palms; we felt engulfed again in the natural pace of life, where time was allowed to follow its course without distortion. Carved wooden doorways, painted in rich mustard yellows, adorned the fronts of rambling houses linked by cobblestones and small decorative gardens. Old women with olive-oil skin and dressed in black purdah, hobbled through the labyrinth and made me think of hillside villages in Crete. We watched the sun set behind the Aga Khan mausoleum, perched on a golden ridge of sand on the opposite side of the river, and the waters of the Nile turned viscous and opalescent as the light faded; it looked infinitely more real than the boulevard behind us.

When Dave and I had first started looking into the idea of cycling through Africa, one piece of information had lodged in my mind: that children throw stones at cyclists in Egypt. We had always joked about this to each other but never considered the reality of it. We were barely five miles out of Aswan and I was dawdling behind the others on the mountain bike. Suddenly a rock, the size of my fist, came flying past my head and skimmed off the tarmac in front. I looked behind to see a teenager, standing thirty yards behind me, grinning with delight; I got the impression that if he had hit me he would be lying on the ground in hysterics. Rather than retaliating, I caught up with the others to tell them.

'Yes, it's true, they do throw stones at you – bloody big stones too.'

'Why, what happened?' asked Chris.

'Some kid just threw a rock at my head, that's what.'

By the end of the day we had encountered three more assailants. One stone had hit Steve on the back and he ran off in pursuit. In a fit of terror the boy had dropped his schoolbooks and disappeared into some fields. Every time we passed through a settlement, which was almost all the time since the road follows the Nile and a continuous stream of villages, we had to be on our guard. Every child, whether in a group or alone, was a potential stone-thrower, and we could see them up ahead searching the ground for suitable ammunition. We did not react kindly to these attacks and, whenever possible, we would try to do something about it. Having cycled over six thousand miles through seven different countries, without one stone being thrown at us, it was doubly exasperating that it should suddenly start happening here in Egypt, a country that *considers* itself to be so much more advanced than its neighbours. These were not isolated incidents; they happened relentlessly every day to such a degree that they considerably hampered our progress and forced us to accept them without retaliation. What we found most difficult to accept was that parents of the children and village elders would look on

without showing any sign of disapproval; only when they saw three
frenzied foreigners chasing children through villages did they realise
that maybe something was wrong. We tried to explain that when
one of their projectiles landed on the exposed cranium of a passing
cyclist, knocking him off the bike and under the wheels of a lorry,
then it was tantamount to murder. However, I do not think that our
rational policy of educating stone-throwers had any effect at all and
my advice to anybody thinking of cycling through Egypt would be
to wear a crash helmet or carry some ammunition of your own.

As anxious as we were to reach Cairo, Luxor could not be seen
in less than two days and we seized the chance of enjoying a respite
from our mounting antipathy for cycling in Egypt. Luxor and Karnak
temples were overwhelming; the sheer monumentality of everything
and the dates involved made my mind reel. Huge bulbous baobab
columns and tapering pylons stood at the gateways with guarding
colossi seated sedately outside. Despite the droves of tourists they
exuded a peaceful eternity. The Valley of the Kings was something
else again – masterpieces of design and craftsmanship carved deep
down into solid rock and leaving no scope for any mistakes. Entering
the first tomb created the most memorable impression – a perfectly
proportioned smooth corridor leading into a sequence of burial
chambers with vaulted ceilings and beautifully sculpted surfaces.
The decorations are immaculately preserved and, where restoration
has occurred, it has been executed with great care and attention to
preserving the original pigments. The predominant colours are a
range of blues, from a deep, almost black lapis, through to a washy
sky blue, a russet-red terracotta, mainly used in the skin of the figures
and a variety of mustard yellows. In some areas a very subtle relief
creates a three dimensional quality; in others a flat, smooth surface
is covered with intricate hieroglyphics.

I could not help reflecting that it seemed sad and strange that the
remnants of such an advanced culture should now be in the hands of a
race who, in our experience, displayed none of the characteristics that
one would associate with such refinement. On our way back to Luxor
we were besieged by people demanding *backsheesh* and asking how
much the trandem cost, a question which had never arisen before.

One cannot attribute this attitude entirely to the corruption brought by tourism because this area has been a major attraction for travellers for over two thousand years.

The following day we battled into a headwind and more flying stones, making a detour from Qena to visit the Dandara temple on the advice of two New Zealand cyclists. They had started cycling north from Aswan but found the headwind too intense, taken a train up to Cairo and headed south. Their experiences of being stoned were similar to ours but made more glamourous by having had one kid pull a gun on them. Dandara proved exceptional – perfectly preserved and the roof still intact. It was built in Greco-Roman times, nearly a thousand years after the Pharaonic temples. A guidebook referred to the workmanship as inferior but I found the rugged, unrefined finish more appealing. The scale of decoration was overwhelming; every wall, door lintel, column and capital is covered in relief sculptures and bold hieroglyphics. The ceilings and some of the rooms resembled beaten bronze due to the dulled, blackish texture, while some rooms were light and showing little trace of the original pigments. Two differently designed staircases with worn, shallow steps led up to the roof – one, a long dark tunnel with small windows throwing shafts of sunlight onto the decorations; the other winding up through separate levels with adjoining rooms. The view from the roof extended down to the sacred lake, the ruins of a Coptic church and the sinuous strata of the encircling wall, with green fields and palm groves stretching to the Nile and mountain ridges beyond.

We continued north through a bleak and flat expanse of pylons. Black clouds swelled out from a factory ahead like escaping demons and I could taste pollution in the air; Africa was behind us. A small complex of shops and a bus stop provided shelter for the night and a genial looking man plied us with food, drinks and *shishas* before producing a highly imaginative bill. He proved more awkward the following morning. After ten miles' cycling, Steve realised that he had left 'the builders' – his shorts – and his 'Cutlers' – sunglasses – behind at the shop. As he explained they were both 'vital pieces of equipment for any discerning expeditioner' and must be retrieved.

Once back at the shop he discovered his shorts mysteriously hidden in a cupboard and devoid of Cutlers.

'Where are my sunglasses?' he demanded.

'Glasses?' answered the shopkeeper with feigned surprise.

'Yes, glasses,' replied Steve emphatically.

After a few feebly acted attempts at looking for them, he looked blankly to Steve and shrugged his shoulders. Steve decided to get angry, issuing ultimatums about their return.

'Ten pounds,' was the bold reply.

'I don't believe this – I am not giving you money for something that belongs to me.'

This dull episode finally concluded without submission to bribery.

Meanwhile, I realised that my passport and wallet were still stashed under the mattress of my bed back in Luxor. Clad in my *galabiyya*, clutching Proust and my sleeping bag, I set off back south. Two official and very silent men in a white jeep took me to the outskirts of Luxor; they chain-smoked the whole way which prompted me to do likewise. Jostling through the narrow streets, ringing with the clamour of the itinerant morning market, I directed positive thoughts towards my wallet, lying precisely where I had left it. To my great relief it was and I promptly dispelled visions of trudging around bastions of bureaucracy in Cairo to try and get a new passport. I celebrated with cups of *kakady* and several *shishas* at our favourite café. The owner, a burly character with a black beard and taunting sense of humour, kept his customers amused as he hovered by the street wielding a huge stick. He looked like one of Ali Baba's forty thieves, straight from the catacombs. It felt good to be alone and I procrastinated over my departure by delving into Proust. Struggling through the more tedious passages earlier in the book was now proving worthwhile – *Time Regained*, the final volume, was sucking me in like a whirlwind as we came closer to the end of our journey. I somehow knew that I would finish the book on arrival in Cairo.

I tend to pride myself on my orientation, discovering shortcuts and finding my way around alien cities. Sometimes however, I go drastically wrong. Trying to get back on the main road outside Luxor was typical of those times. My route somehow took me a few

kilometres round three walls of the Karnak temple before crossing
massive irrigation ditches and scrambling through thickets into the
backyards of houses and confronting the bewildered occupants. The
sight of a dishevelled, barefoot European tumbling through thorn
bushes in a filthy *galabiyya* must have come as a surprise. One hour
later I found the road, where I was picked up by a genial man driving
a lorry full of glass. My extremely limited grasp of Arabic and his
non-existent English led to a silent journey up to Sohag.

Sohag boasted the most beautiful cafés we had seen. Abundant
mirrors and marble floors made me think of coffee houses in Vienna.
The others drew into town an hour later, exasperated by another
day of stoning. A young student, who had pestered me since my
arrival, now made the mistake of asking Chris how he enjoyed
Egypt. A torrent of invective poured forth which wiped the smile
off his face and sent him on his way. Dave was on the verge of
collapse; strange things were brewing in his stomach so we went in
search of a hotel. He was even worse the next morning and decided
to hitch on to Asyut.

We were three days from Cairo and the mounting adrenalin added
impetus to the cycling. Ninety miles in a day, even with two of us on
the trandem, felt quite manageable. Little was said about the brewing
excitement. The stone-throwers had bred a pervasive antipathy in us;
it was now a question of heads down and burn up those miles. There
were other incidents every day which fuelled our mounting distrust.
Twenty miles from Asyut we pulled over for some tea. The inevitable
crowd of children gathered round the bikes and started to fiddle. In
disbelief I watched one boy open up a pannier and, right in front of
me, pull two cassettes from the top and stuff them in his pocket. He
did not even attempt to conceal what he was doing. I was livid. I stood
up, grabbed him by the neck and hit him. This in turn enraged an
adult standing nearby and a furious row broke out. This man spoke
good English, was clearly well educated, but could not understand
why I was so angry.

'But this boy was stealing from us.'

'No, no, no.'

'Yes, yes, yes. He just opened this and put these in his pocket.'

'No, no, no.'

'I don't believe this – let's go.'

Asyut is the fundamentalist centre of Egypt. Incidents like this became noticeably more aggressive and more frequent – the same day Chris and Steve had chased some stone-throwers off the road and into a house. I stayed with the bikes, bored by the delays now incurred by these attacks and the reprisals. Thirty seconds later they came running back out of the house, hotly pursued by four men brandishing six-foot wooden poles above their heads. Chris called for his nunchukkas as he was knocked to the ground by severe blows to the back of his head. I had just pulled our weapons from the front of the bike when two elders rushed up and pacified the most potentially violent encounter of the year. These two old men apologised profusely as we tried to contain the heated abuse which flowed spontaneously on these occasions.

Dave's plan was to collapse in the hotel closest to the station in Asyut. We found him easily. He had a fever, severe stomach cramps and looked several pounds thinner than he had that morning. A doctor had made an obscure diagnosis and prescribed some very odd drugs which only seemed to make him worse. We came across a medical student in the café below who was determined to give him a course of injections. As I was to discover later, this is the course of action taken by Egyptian doctors in absolutely any circumstance – your complaint can be anything from a sore throat to a broken leg and they will reach for the needle. Also in the café we met a young Coptic student. From a distance he looked like an albino but close up we realised that he had unusually fair skin and almost golden hair. His shy, peaceful approach was refreshing. We spent most of the evening with him and heard some disturbing stories. Two weeks ago one of his friends, another Christian, had organised a coach trip down to Luxor for some of the students. Men and women had not been divided into different buses. This had provoked some extremists to such an extent that they beat him to death with bicycle chains. Only one week before a Coptic church had been burnt down. Being white was synonymous with being Christian, and that was why we were being harassed.

By the next morning Dave had received prescriptions from three different doctors, each of whom presented a new diagnosis. Completely confused, he decided to try all three remedies at the same time. Leaving him to catch the train, we arranged to meet two days later in Beni Suef. Steve, Chris and I pushed on as fast as possible through the relentless roadside bombardment. Refusing to break our pace and rhythm, the culprits were ignored as much as possible. The road remained straight and flat, and the traffic increased as the urban sprawl swallowed up more of the landscape. My perception of natural beauty had been displaced by antipathy bordering on hatred, compounded by our level of physical exertion. My thoughts never deviated from the final pages of Proust or the mental picture of our arrival in Cairo. I was deeply immersed in time but heading for something outside it.

The main square in Beni Suef struck me as unusually mellow. Exhausted from a fast ride over eighty-five miles, we slumped down in the nearest café and ordered cups of tea. I was feeling relaxed with our surroundings for the first time in days and even remarked: 'I quite like Beni Suef.'

Suddenly I felt a tap on my shoulder and heard a voice say, 'Hello Mister.' I turned to reply. A young man of about twenty stood before me, holding a dustbin and grinning from ear to ear. He then emptied rubbish all over me before planting the bin firmly on my head. I was so stupefied by this bizarre form of greeting, I just sat there in darkness. By the time I had registered what was happening he had disappeared and other men in the café blocked our attempts to chase him. I was so angry that I started shaking. I could hardly speak for the next five minutes. Never had I witnessed or been subjected to such an absurd confrontation. The pure madness of it, however, forced me to wind down and by the time Dave arrived, twenty minutes later, we were laughing about it.

Seeking seclusion in a hotel, I spent the whole evening writing about Islam. How could the people of two neighbouring Muslim areas like Egypt and northern Sudan be so completely different? Is industrial development and western materialism entirely to blame or is the rise of Islamic fundamentalism at the root of this disturbing attitude towards foreigners? At the end of the day I could only conclude that it was.

The thought of missing the last day's ride into Cairo would have been too much for any of us to contemplate, regardless of physical condition. Dave was feeling more normal and we left Beni Suef at full strength. All the traffic in Africa seemed to funnel together in one blaring convoy as Cairo came closer. Every truck insisted on blasting its horn for five seconds as it came up behind us and the entire day was spent in a black cloud of exhaust fumes. A wide dual carriageway emerged and with it the industrial shanty-towns of suburban Cairo – a grey and polluted vision of mechanical carnage next to streams of noxious chemical waste. Broken spokes on the freewheel side taunted our patience as the adrenalin flowed. Although we only had ten miles left to cycle, we knew that the rim would buckle if we did not replace them. Pulling over to dismantle the wheel, I could smell the frustration as everybody did their utmost to keep cool. I smoked five cigarettes.

Half an hour later the skyscrapers of central Cairo loomed out of the smog ahead and a sense of triumph surged through my mind like a rush of ecstasy. The consummation of a one-year daydream, nurtured over six thousand miles, unleashed waves of bottled emotion and we began to sing.

Following the Nile into the city, we stopped on one of the bridges to decide what to do next; we could hardly afford a beer between us, let alone champagne; we knew that the cheapest hotel in Cairo was called the Oxford, it was nearly dusk and we probably ought to start looking for it. The singing had stopped. The euphoria had gone. That was that – a five-minute buzz which would never return.

Depression followed. I read the final pages of Proust and closed a chapter of my life. The incessant cacophony of Cairo filled the air that I breathed but never permeated the internal world where I was living, displaced and outside time. Reality came through shuttered windows in dusty beams of morning sun.

I awoke the following morning with a pain in my groin. My right testicle was red and swollen. I shrugged it off as something caused by hard cycling and an uncomfortable saddle. By the following morning it was twice the size and twice as painful; walking without discomfort required a degree of care. By the third day it was the size of a tennis ball and I was walking like a bow-legged John Wayne. On the same day, it just so happened that our contact in the British Embassy had organised for us to go round the Pyramids – on horses. I had never sat on a horse in my life and nothing was going to make me start now. I politely declined her invitation, due to 'some pain in a sensitive area' and, much to my amusement, watched the others saddle up and disappear into the dunes. Rather relieved that I could enjoy the pyramids on my own, I hobbled up a rocky outcrop on the nearest dune. It was a misty morning which, combined with the smog, made visibility poor. However, I was determined to use the self-timer to photograph myself sitting serenely on this rock, gazing romantically towards the Great Pyramid. After trying various positions, I placed the camera on a ledge about ten feet behind the crest of the ridge. To get myself into frame I had to drop six feet down from the camera, walk three yards and then climb six feet onto the rock. I set the focus and aperture and started the self-timer. With extreme caution I lowered myself down, waddled across the gap and started scrabbling up to my position. I was just sitting down when I heard the beep and the click of the shutter. I tried again and the same thing happened. This ludicrous pursuit of vanity went on for half an hour and wasted half a roll of film. Rather than the romantic image expected, I ended up with nearly twenty photographs of my backside poised over the lip of a rock.

The next morning I tottered slowly to the nearest hospital. After half an hour I was led into a surgery and asked to lie down. The doctor was staggered to hear that I had cycled from Botswana to Cairo and quite understandably diagnosed my complaint as a bruised testicle caused by sitting on a saddle for most of the year. A course of injections over the next week was apparently what I needed. I explained that we were flying to Milan in two days but succumbed to the first injection and returned to the hotel.

The Oxford Pension sat at the top of a six-storey building. Fortunately the lift was working. A steady stream of the lowest budget travellers passed through and there was always an interesting collection of people to talk to. The noise pollution in Cairo is unbelievable – sixty-five per cent of the population take sedatives to sleep. Some residents at the Oxford were trying to override this by attempting to sleep through the day and stay up drinking at night when the decibel levels were down. Everybody looked equally exasperated by the city, hanging out for a flight to Europe or a bus going south. The hotel reception was like a room full of disturbed mental patients waiting to be discharged. By the end of the week I was so immobile that I stayed up late every night with Dave and a German called Andreas. He was our age and a most unusual character, claiming to have been born with an overload of endorphines. He had read everything under the sun and kept us fascinated with his repertoire of bizarre stories about harvest parties at Ken Kesey's farm in Oregon. His extensive travels seemed to be funded by the LSD he transported all over the globe.

Leaving Cairo was more of a release than an emotional farewell. I travelled by taxi to the airport, senses nullified by the brewing pain between my legs.

And then there was one . . .

My Italian godfather was the complete antithesis of what this *mafioso* title might suggest. He was the most generous and charming man that I have ever had the good fortune to know, let alone have as a godfather. Whenever the going got tough during the year I had distracted the others with references to 'Papa Nunzio and his *palazzo* on Lake Como'. By now we had all developed such an opulent vision of our arrival in Europe that to be denied it would have been devastating. I had tried to contact Nunzio from Cairo but without success. The possibility of him being away started to worry me intensely but I did not have the heart to tell the others.

Milan airport made us all rather bemused – the frantic speed at which everybody was hurtling around and doing things in a pristine ordered environment was a positively alien experience. The twenty-first century seemed to have arrived in our absence. After battling with the instructions on a payphone, I put a call through to Nunzio. There was no reply. The pain in my nether regions had subsided and I decided to cycle into town on the mountain bike without actually sitting on the saddle. This proved very exhausting. Two hours later we were still riding around Milan, inquiring about cheap hotels and stopping at call-boxes. Money from the fifty-pound travellers' cheque which I had cashed at the airport was dwindling rapidly and would only cover two of us for a bed that night. Some teenagers passing in a car tried to help us out but could only suggest heading for a bridge where the tramps slept. I tried Nunzio again; no reply. On the off-chance, I tried the house in Orvieto where he used to live. A familiar voice answered.

'Pronto.'

'Nunzio, it's Rory.'

'Aaah Rary, where are you?' he asked in his endearing Italian accent.

'Well, we're in Milan actually and we were wondering if you could suggest a cheap hotel for us to go to.'

'Now Rary, you must go, Via Torino, to the Hotel Ascot and I will pay the bill.'

'No, no Nunzio . . .'

'I will ring them now and call me when you get there.'

The Hotel Ascot proved to be a five-star concrete palace. I rang Nunzio back and explained that we should be going to the cheapest hostel in town but he was having none of it.

'Now Rary, you must go, Ristorante Smeraldino, Porta Garibaldi, ask for Mario, and Rary I want you to go there as many times as you like until I come to Milano.'

None of us could grasp the reality of the situation. Wearing the tattered remains of our collective wardrobe, we shuffled in disbelief to our rooms, led by porters dressed in their finest livery and carrying luggage smeared with bicycle grease. Steve and I just collapsed into hysterics at the sight of our room. I wandered into the bathroom, picked up a large white bath towel, pressed it against my face and started groaning as I hugged it. Ten minutes later a half-bottle of champagne appeared in each room and hysterics continued. By now I was oblivious to pain and the swelling seemed to have gone down.

The Porta Garibaldi was on the other side of town so I asked reception for a taxi – the evening had to continue in style. Because we were staying at a luxury hotel and wearing such ridiculous clothes, our taxi driver immediately assumed that we were a band. He turned to Steve, who was wearing his bright green embroidered *galabiyya* and was sitting in the passenger seat.

'So, you play guitar?'

'Well, as it happens . . .'

'I knew it – I am musician too – you must join me later at this bar – very good . . .' and so he went on, hardly pausing for breath and hardly looking at the road, bouncing up and down on his seat and frothing at the mouth like an archetypal speed freak.

Ristorante Smeraldino is the most fashionable restaurant in town, packed with Milano supermodels. The entire place fell silent as we walked in. I asked for Mario and we were ushered through a sea of bewildered faces to our table. The state of shock surrounding us subsided as we ploughed into the *antipasto* and bottles of Barolo. By the end of the first course we had all fallen in love with the same waitress. By the end of the main course we were determined to go out clubbing. Popular opinion directed us to a club on the opposite side of Porta Garibaldi. Without a penny between us we walked to the front of the queue and explained ourselves to the doorman. He told us to talk to the boss, a young man who came walking up the stairs.

'Hi, we've just cycled through Africa on a bicycle with three seats and we have just arrived in Milan and we really want to go into your club and if we can we'll mention it in our book which we are going to write when we get back.' This garbled tirade must have made an impression.

'It's my birthday, it's OK, in you go.'

Not only did he let us in for free, he then came down and bought us all champagne. Euphoria and intoxication ensued as we danced like dervishes for two hours. Sitting down for a cigarette in an alcove beside the dancefloor, I suddenly saw this six-foot blonde model come rushing up towards me. I braced myself. She grabbed the hem of my *galabiyya*, looked up at me and in a thick American accent said 'Geee, I love this, where d'ya git it? Is it Gaultier?'

Whether it was the abundance of beautiful girls or the manic dancing that was responsible for the return of my malady I do not know, but I woke the next morning with a bollock bigger than a baked potato. My hunchback stature and splayed gait returned as we wandered between the hotel and the restaurant for the one meal a day I had allowed at Nunzio's expense. We began to realise just how strange we looked because we caused such consternation amongst passers-by. People on the other side of the street would actually stop and gawp at us.

On the third day Nunzio returned to Milan. Next thing we knew we were gliding along the motorway to Como in his Rolls-Royce. I knew that 'Papa Nunzio's *palazzo*' was not going to be small but I

had never envisaged the grandeur that awaited us. Sitting right on
the lake, serene and classical, it was more of a paradise in every way
than any of us had imagined. The lake itself is enclosed by plunging
prehistoric mountains which make one feel isolated, above the world
around. The rooms are cool and spacious with a Zen-like minimalism.
Blue marble mosaics made the floor a pure sensation after stepping
from the heat outside.

Our days at Como started late. Cups of strong black coffee soon
merged into glasses of chilled Riesling and a long lunch. It was a new
and different world. We drifted about the house in our *galabiyyas*,
soaking up every second. As the days passed the baked potato grew
and the pain increased, stretching right up into my stomach. By
the third day I was unable to sleep at night. The only relief came
from sitting in hot baths so my nights were spent curled up on the
bathroom floor, running hot baths and sitting in them until the water
was cold. After two sleepless nights I acknowledged that something
was seriously wrong and that I should see a doctor. The idea of not
being able to cycle the last stretch back to London, an ambition
which had been nurtured for over a year, had prevented me from
accepting this before. My vision of the end of the journey had always
been Chelsea and not Cairo.

I explained my embarrassing predicament to Nunzio and we
set off for the hospital in Como. The doctor's examination was
excruciatingly painful but extremely amusing at the same time.
Nunzio had to act as interpreter as I lay on a couch and the
doctor prodded my balls. It was a surreal nightmare. With every
prod I sat bolt upright and screamed before falling back in hysterics.
Intermittent screaming and laughter continued for twenty minutes
before the doctor concluded that I should return to London as soon
as possible.

The next few days were weird. The disappointment completely
overshadowed any fear of what might be wrong with me. I had such
a concrete idea of how we would return to London and it had been
shattered so suddenly. Nunzio took me to the airport and bought
me a ticket. I stumbled through Immigration in a daze and waited
for the flight to be called. The space-age environment of the airport

disturbed me. There was an abundance of unnecessary technology everywhere – TV monitors telling me what the temperature had been in Helsinki at 4.40 the previous afternoon and what the time was in Tokyo. I wondered why I would need to know this, and even if I did, why it needed to be on ten different screens in the same place at the same time. I pondered over this as I got to the front of the queue for boarding. I handed my boarding card to an efficient looking hostess.

'Could you wait over there please sir.'

'Why?' I asked rather belligerently.

'You're Business Class sir.'

Nunzio had bought a Business Class ticket without me knowing. I shuffled awkwardly towards a group of twenty chic Milano businessmen clutching briefcases and reading newspapers. I noticed looks of disdain and incredulity. The seat of my trousers had long since disappeared, exposing some tattered shorts beneath, and my luggage consisted of a decomposing sleeping bag hanging from a pannier covered in bicycle grease. My neighbour on the plane actually asked if he could sit somewhere else.

Back in London I was whisked to the Lister hospital and plugged into lots of expensive hardware. A tumour was diagnosed and my right testicle was removed. Five days later it was found to be benign and I was in the clear. Those five days had a profound impact on me because I had never confronted the idea of my death so closely. I found myself clinging desperately to Nature, to the light dancing on spring blossoms and budding trees at my father's house. Then I realised that I did not matter because I am part of that. I am a part of One thing and what matters is that Oneness.

Epilogue

Nature had fuelled me throughout Africa and I felt fortunate. She had made me happier and more balanced than ever before in my life, but was now to make me miserable and moralistic. I became morbidly preoccupied with the destruction of the planet, critical of everybody around me, cynical of what propelled them and depressed with my inability to transcend the mundane, the superficial and material. I knew that certain compromises could never be made without living with a perpetual lie.

One might think that my cycling days were over. However, I was back on the trandem within weeks, finding freedom from the stagnant environment of London whenever I rode her. Within months Steve and I were planning other journeys but these floundered when he announced that he was going to study accountancy in Norwich – a radical decision at the best of times. A variety of routes and plans flourished for a few days at a time before finding their way back into the obscurity and absurdity which had conceived them. Perhaps the most ambitious of these was a proposal to ride the trandem '. . . on the golden road to Samarkand with a blind man at the helm'.

Dave became a mountain bike fanatic. He rapidly convinced a friend to invest in mountain bike holidays and formed a company called 'Intrepid Trips', a name coined from Ken Kesey's Merry Pranksters. Soon he was back in his beloved Africa, researching routes in the Atlas mountains of Morocco. Intrepid Trips existed for two years, operated successfully during that time but failed to provide the financial rewards required. In 1992 they sold the company to a large adventure travel specialist, where Dave now runs the show on a handsome salary. During this time the equipment manager's dimples, bold charisma and supreme knowledge of bicycle technology, led to him appearing on the *Mountain Bike Show*, every week giving maintenance tips as The Grease Monkey, a source of considerable amusement for the rest of us. Meanwhile Chris was developing his *penchant* for malt whisky, working for a wine merchant in Soho.

I spent all the money I could muster on buying a computer and, based at my father's house, started to work on this book. From the start I knew that I was not really a writer. Although my efforts to film the trip through Africa had been nothing short of disastrous, I was still determined to pursue documentary film production as a career. I bluffed my way into showing some embarrassingly dodgy footage to someone at Channel 4, who was predictably unimpressed but put me in touch with a young producer/director who was to become the first of several important contacts that ultimately led to the production of my first film out in India in 1993. To make the film I set up a small independent production company, ONE Productions, with Matthew Whitley, an old friend who had worked in film production for a few years. The film follows a journey made by Bill Oddie, Cyrung (a six-foot-six Australian didgeridoo-player) and I, travelling along the Ganges on the Goodloid, taking Bill to the spot where his best friend had been killed by a tiger ten years previously. I instigated the trip as a way to draw attention to various environmental issues, in particular the pollution problem in the river. Through the sale of the film around the world we plan to generate funds for a pressure group in Varanasi called 'Swatcha Ganga', which has been instrumental in persuading the government to activate an ambitious plan to clean up the river.

Five years have elapsed since our return from Africa and all the time it becomes easier to put the experiences of the year into context. For the first couple of years the loss of my right testicle seemed to be synonymous with a loss of masculinity; I felt empty, hollow and half-male. Now I treat it as a symbolic sacrifice to Nature, an acceptable price to pay for what She had given me. Sleeping in the bush by night and drifting through it by day, carried by the meditative motion of the Goodloid, brought me closer to a dimension which had always been of interest but which has subsequently become of paramount importance. I really believe that I did leave parts of my self behind in Africa, that I started opening to a process which is gathering momentum all the time – a process of gradual transformation, a shedding of the false self, a dismantling of the ego as the true self struggles to shine through.

The pessimistic contempt I felt upon our return – for patriarchal western values, for the expansionist greed which is plundering and destroying the fragile ecosystems of the planet, for the disastrous developments occurring throughout the world in the name of progress, for the spiritually barren society in which we live – all of this has gradually been replaced by a fresh optimism. I now believe that human consciousness keeps evolving, that throughout history there have been significant shifts in the direction of consciousness brought about by the forces that created and sustain the world in which we live. We are all a part of the One, one self-regulating organism being knocked off-balance by greed. The fundamental restructuring of world economics, which is essential if we are going to have any chance of preserving what remains of our beautiful planet, can only be made possible by the spiritual transformation of human consciousness. I believe that this transformation has already started. For me, this is the beginning.

And Finally . . .

Dave

Three Men on a Bike was undoubtedly one of the most foolish, ambitious and extraordinary ideas I have ever been party to creating, let alone carrying out. Despite this it was certainly one of the best!

From the moment I sat on a mountain bike for the first time in Oxford, in 1988, I knew this trip was something that I needed to do, even if I didn't know how at the time. Strangely, I also felt quite convinced that something would come out of the trip, though no one, let alone me, thought it would be a career designing and organising cycling holidays!

I found the cycling to be not only challenging, but invigorating and rewarding to the extent where it has almost created a rebirth of my mind and body. The brotherhood the bike brought with the Africans and their land was so wonderful, that my work now tries to reflect this, albeit through tourism. To this day, I continue to find that just riding a bike frees my mind and allows me to think in a way that is not normally possible; it is an emancipating experience that lets my mind roam free, like the endless horizons of Africa. I am only amazed (and saddened) that none of the others have ever really sat on a bike since, though each to their own, and perhaps the bike was a different type of vehicle to them.

Life on the road, living in nature was such a beautiful and unconfused experience. The simplicity of living a primeval life where our only concerns were: where to sleep safely, where the next food and water would come from, and how to get to London (God knows

I will never have a goal to get there again), was one I shall probably never experience so fully again.

Through all our problems it was this simplicity of life and purpose that made the trip possible. Similarly the spirit of the African people and the ability of my colleagues to laugh and party, regardless of circumstance, gave the journey and us our fulfilment.

A Word on Europe . . . Rory's sudden departure in Italy was a real blow to the team and I still cannot comprehend how difficult it must have been for him to fly back to England, unannounced, to face an operation that would make any man quake. As the three people who had shared a unique world with him for a year, our separation from him at the time of the 'great cultural divide' will never be underestimated.

Cycling in Europe consequently started off with a very strange vibe, which became a reality when Papa Nunzio dropped us in Milan to pick up the Goodloid. Returning his cashmere sweaters, we donned garbage bags, over shorts and T-shirts, to protect us from the rain and headed out to cross the snow-covered Alps.

In keeping with the rest of the year, we had very little money and couldn't afford to stay anywhere, resorting to going to the cheapest hotels, explaining our predicament and asking if we could sleep in their garages. To epitomise the European stage, on one occasion, a certain Swiss hotelier was so generous he allowed us this privilege for a mere £5 a head, and we spent a night in sub-zero temperatures wrapped up in discarded, used carpeting from the hotel lavatories.

We crossed the Alps between Switzerland and France in a snow storm and it was so cold that we had to wear our only pair of socks as gloves in order to prevent frostbite and enable us to operate the brakes. In addition, the pedals had been bent from hitting submerged rocks in the desert and the combination of this, the alpine passes and sub-zero temperatures rapidly annihilated my knees.

As we continued into France my knees got worse and worse and soon I could hardly walk, whilst Steve and Chris stepped up the pace to 'escape from Europe'. I was forced to resort to catching buses and meeting the others in the evening, having spent the day applying tinctures and eating anti-inflammatories in the hope of riding the following day. The disappointment of cycling all the way across Africa and then my body failing me on the home straight was immense and with Rory gone and African hospitality replaced by European fear of the unknown, the celebratory return envisaged in Africa now looked bleak. Finally, having missed the last few days to Calais, I was allowed to steer the bike off the ferry back onto English soil, before being virtually carried through the streets of Dover to our lodgings.

Arriving back in London on the 10.30 from Dover simply was not the same as arriving on the Goodloid, and as Rory and I waited for Steve and Chris I felt (God knows what Rory felt) I had been denied some right that I had earned. However in time I have come to realise that our reward had nothing to do with cycling those last miles up the King's Road. For neither London, Europe nor any numerical calculation of distance is important, only the experience. The Goodloid made it and in her oneness so did we.

I wouldn't swop the experience for anything and I can only hope that in my lifetime I might one day do something else which I will appreciate as much as this. Maybe it's time for the three men to ride again?

Steve

Dave asked me recently why I went to Africa. This is quite hard to answer. In those few moments at Tom's house when the idea was unfolded I realised that it was an opportunity to do something completely special. It was unique. Here was something that was going to be a first – an attempt to accomplish something genuinely difficult – a physical, mental and mechanical challenge. I could live out my boyhood fantasies, have an adventure and recount the tales to my grandchildren.

To say that the experience changed my life is more than an understatement. As Rory rightly points out, Africa wasn't merely about taking on experience – it was a mutual exchange. The vast continent pulsating in ancient and untouched harmony retains our laughter, sweat and tears. (And no doubt half of our blood in obscure and isolated malaria clinics.)

When I returned to England, witnessing a glorious sunset over the White Cliffs of Dover with Chris, I felt incredibly alive. I'd managed to get a glimpse of something that will resonate within me for the rest of my life. I was also slightly confused, and retired to the seclusion of a hillside cottage in Wales to write songs and to try and work out what to do next.

I was acutely aware that I wanted to use this regained sense of energy and ambition which seemed to have been destroyed by three years at university, so decided to embark on a professional career after tying up the loose ends of the trip.

I wanted to do law but found it impossible to get onto a conversion course. I worked in a fashionable London wine bar and played gigs whenever I could as well as writing and performing the music for a half-hour film at the London International Film School.

After six months in London I felt terrible. I was broke, unhealthy and had split up with Emily. I remember vividly languishing in a basement in Notting Hill watching the Gulf War twenty-four hours a day. My depression pervaded everything. Finally, I decided that this had to stop.

I'd obviously gone slightly insane, because I left for Norwich, to escape . . . and do accountancy. Although I value what I learnt, I hated accountancy and after two years finally secured a place on a conversion course to do law.

Since then I've regained an inner peace. I look forward as well as back and feel comforted that Africa gave me an inner strength. It also gave me three friendships I know I shall never lose.

Chris

There were times when all I could think of was why on earth was I here in the middle of Africa on a bike that should have been in a museum? On reflection, I would not have wanted to be anywhere else. It all began with a phone-call.

'Hi Chris, Dave here . . . Listen, Rory and I want to come over and see you at lunchtime – we have a proposition for you.'

I knew their game of course. The African trip idea had done the rounds, everyone including myself had had a good laugh at Dave and Rory's expense and I had absolutely no intention of succumbing to their ludicrous ploy. However, it was another boring day in Peckham and I needed an excuse to get out of my dingy prison of an office . . . so we agreed to meet.

Lunch was a pub affair, my morning having been spent plotting lines of defence on why I could not possibly join them on such a madcap trip that I deemed was doomed to failure. Within ten minutes my defence lines had been breached, the trenches overrun and I had surrendered . . . and signed up.

All they had said was true – yes, my job as an estate agent was exceptionally dull. Yes, the housing market had just lurched and tumbled from its inflated position and no, the prospects of gainful employment as a negotiator were not looking good. Finally, yes I would undoubtedly prefer to be in Africa than Peckham. That afternoon I consoled myself that it was a mad idea, conceived by mad men and that it would surely never materialise. As it turned out these men were obsessed – they were the epitome of Lawrence's 'dangerous dreamers of the day' and so we arrived in Botswana.

We were probably the most clueless expedition team ever to have undergone such a trip with only a smattering of bike maintenance skills between us, although we did carry a copy of the Readers Digest manual of bike maintenance, and had a semblance of fitness. How did we make it? Well, I put it down to a mixture of bloody-mindedness, lunacy and a healthy dose of good humour. Was I a changed man for the trip? I have changed and I know I will never be the same again.

I remember how overwhelmed I felt by our arrival in Botswana as it was the first time I had a chance to understand the magnitude of our undertaking. On our second night I experienced the hollowness of staring down the barrel of a grenade launcher, but the greatest experience from the outset was the indeterminate feeling of space and freedom.

I have been fascinated and magnetically drawn to water ever since I can remember, consequently my favourite memories of Africa all revolve around the areas we visited with plenty of water. I was awestruck by the 'musi o tunya', or thunderous sound of the Zambesi. Lake Malawi was a paradise unparalleled in my experience. It was our mother and life, its tranquil waters blew four months of travel away and, although it was the first time we struck malaria, it was a grind to tear ourselves away. The Indian Ocean seemed to herald the end of what seemed a lifetime of travel and our time spent at Christmas on Lamu was as excessive as any I have experienced. My diary entry for our Christmas dinner is as follows ... '3 fillets of tuna fried with curry, 2 kilos of prawns boiled with lemons, 3 lobsters with a stilton sauce, 20 curried eggs, tomato and onion salad with a lemon dressing, potato salad, lightly boiled cabbage, bread and 5 litres of heinously strong cocktail'.

The Sudan was a revelation. The Northern Sudanese were hospitable beyond comprehension – a far cry from the international pariah that it has for a Government. They are unspoilt by tourism, poor, unimposing in their religious beliefs and the only people I can imagine who look distinctly noble sitting on donkeys. And then there is the Nile – the colour of algae a permanent cool oasis threading through an endless desolate moonscape – it again was our mother and life. I remember waking early one morning and sauntering off alone to sit on the bank. Huge fish swirled, thrashed and slurped things noisily off the surface while I sat and pondered. It was as if my life suddenly made sense.

When we left the Sudan, the trip took on a new dimension – the flight home. Rory has made it plain how we were treated there and I will not dwell ... except to say that I began to understand the origin of the saying 'giving someone some gyp'. Straight out of Egypt, Europe was a test on our resolve. Dave's knees packed up mid-way across France and it was left to Steve and I to steer the bike home and at the same time we notched up the longest ride in a day, 103 miles. When we arrived at the finish line at World's End in the King's Road, all we could think of was turning around and starting again.